NOTRE DAME DU HAUT
1950–54
GUGGENHEIM MUSEUM
1956–59
TWA TERMINAL
1956–62
CONGRESS BUILDING
BRASÍLIA
1958–60
SYDNEY OPERA HOUSE
1957–73
OLYMPIC PARK IN
MUNICH
1968–72
JEWISH MUSEUM
BERLIN
1992–99
NATIONAL STADIUM IN
BEIJING
2003–08

TAJ MAHAL
1632–52
POTALA PALACE
FROM 17TH C
VERSAILLES
FROM 1668
ZWINGER PALACE
1709–28
UPPER BELVEDERE
1721–23
THE LOUVRE
FROM 12TH C
MONTICELLO
CA. 1770
ROYAL CRESCENT
1767–74

UNITED STATES CAPITOL
FROM 1793
LA SAGRADA FAMÍLIA
FROM 1882
THE EIFFEL TOWER
1887–89
SULLIVAN CENTER
1899–1904
BAUHAUS
1925–26
CHRYSLER BUILDING
1928–30
CASA MALAPARTE
1938–43
THE GLASS HOUSE
1947–49

1632–1757

1793–1947

1950–2003

50 BUILDINGS

YOU SHOULD KNOW

Isabel Kuhl

PRESTEL

Munich · London · New York

CONTENTS

01

THE GREAT PYRAMID OF GIZA

Pharaoh Khufu's tomb on the west bank of the River Nile was quite simply the largest construction in the ancient world. The pharaoh made no attempt to be modest – the most impressive of the Egyptian pyramids soars 146 metres (478 feet) above the ground.

The Great Pyramid of Giza, Egypt
2554–2531 BC

FACT FILE

Location South-west of Cairo
Height Almost 147 m / 482 ft
(today 138.8 m / 455 ft)
Length of side 230 m / 755 ft
(today 225 m / 738 ft)
Area of base Approx. 53,000 sq m /
570,486 sq ft
Area of surface 85,500 sq m /
920,310 sq ft
Materials Limestone, basalt and
granite
Number of stone blocks Approx.
2.5 million
Estimated total weight Approx.
6.35 million tons

In the third millennium BC, an entire necropolis spread over Giza, on the border with the Libyan Desert. Pharaoh Khufu (Cheops) built his own final resting place on a rock plateau 40 metres (130 feet) high only a few kilometres south-west of present-day Cairo. His father, Snofru, had already inaugurated the period of the major royal buildings: so far, more than 80 pyramids have been discovered in the Nile Valley. The Great Pyramid can be seen from a great distance, rising above the flat, desert landscape. Khufu's burial complex as a whole covers an area of over one square kilometre (about 240 acres) and is surrounded by hundreds of additional graves of his queens and important officials.

Decades of Stone upon Stone

A great many craftsmen and labourers worked for almost 30 years on Khufu's pyramid, living to the west of the building site in a temporary village. Between 2554 and 2531 BC they cut, moved and set in place 2.5 million large stone blocks to form a pyramid 210 stone courses high. Only 201 of them have survived until today as the pyramids not only fell victim to the wind and rain, but were also used by the Romans as a ready supply of building material. At the time of construction, around 5,000 stonemasons worked in the quarries to provide the rock and limestone and then build the pyramid. If the thousands of transport workers and servants are included, approximately 20,000 to 25,000 people were occupied with the construction of the Great Pyramid – one percent of the total Egyptian population of the period.

Superb Feat of Engineering

The Egyptians had acquired an extremely sophisticated building technology and advanced mathematical knowledge. The country's architects had no difficulty in calculating volumes, areas and angles with great precision, even though they used simple tools. Starting from the square base, the smooth surfaces of the pyramid's sides converge to form four triangles that meet at its peak. In spite of the sides having a base length of 230 metres (755 feet), the divergences in the construction of the pyramid are limited to a few centimetres.

Gigantic stone blocks were transported to the very centre of the construction to form the grave chamber that was to house the sarcophagus containing the embalmed body of the pharaoh. A low, sloping passageway leads downwards from the northern entrance to a large hall, where three enormous stone blocks protected the grave chamber from intruders. It was necessary to take great pains when constructing this chamber, which measures 10 x 20 Egyptian ells – or 5.2 x 10.45 metres (17 x 34 feet) – as the Egyptians believed that the pharaoh lived on eternally in his pyramid. It was also hoped that he would take care of his people from the afterlife. For this reason, he had to be well provided for: fresh air came through slender shafts, exquisite burial goods were stacked around his sarcophagus, and sacrifices were offered up to him in the Temple of the Dead at the foot of the pyramid. His happiness ensured the happiness of Egypt.

Chephren's Pyramid in the foreground with the Pyramid of Khufu behind it.

next pages: The Sphinx, with the Great Pyramid of Giza in the background

02

KARNAK TEMPLE

The Egyptian kingdom reached the height of its power during the second millennium BC. The country on the Nile had become the major power in the region. The New Kingdom demonstrated this power and wealth through the building of gigantic temple complexes, the finest of which are Luxor, Abu Simbel and the temple at Karnak.

Karnak Temple, Egypt

FACT FILE

Location 3 kilometres north of Luxor
Size of the entire enclosure 250,000 sq m / 2,690,978 sq ft
Size of the Amun District 530 x 510 x 510 x 700 m / 1738.10 x 1673.3 x 1673.3 x 2296.7 ft
Maximum width of the pylon 110 m / 360.10 ft
Maximum height of the pylon 40 m / 131.3 ft

In the years between 1551 and 715 BC, the Nile valley took on a new appearance. Walled temple complexes of enormous size were erected in honour of the gods and the pharaohs. In Karnak, north-east of Luxor on the right bank of the Nile, tribute was paid to Amun, the sun god, one of the most revered Egyptian deities. Numerous rulers were to be involved before the temple complex, which was begun around 1550 BC, reached its final colossal size.

The temple itself rises from a rectangular base and is surrounded by massive walls. The entrance front is decorated with monumental columns and gate towers called pylons. These serve as the entrance to the temple, and are followed by a courtyard with colonnades on both sides. A spacious, covered, columned hall was connected to a second pylon. The diameter of the supports, lined up close together in rows of three, is enormous. The column shafts and capitals are decorated with figures and vegetal ornaments. Sunlight flows into the interior through openings at the side. Additional anterooms and pylons lead into the sanctuary: the great temple of Amun with its effigy of the god.

The Temple of Temples

During the New Kingdom there was a passion for building. This becomes obvious at Karnak, where entire generations of rulers made additions. Numerous forecourts, pylons and temples, huge sculptures and obelisks, were erected. The construction received its first major enlargement during the reign of Thutmosis I, whose daughter then donated the obelisks for her father's additions. Thutmosis III added an additional magnificent columned hall in the south-west of the complex, where he was worshipped more than the god. Ramses II also could not resist making a contribution of this kind, and added a similar hall and monumental sculptures. The list goes on and on. The basic temple type of the New Kingdom was fully realized in the Amun Temple in Karnak, and in gargantuan dimensions. Processions entered through the monumental gates and proceeded along the long axis of the temple: many of the rituals of such processions are immortalized in stone on the columns in the halls of the temple.

Notwithstanding the building passion of the Pharaohs, which was often self-serving, Karnak had one ultimate goal: for the sake of the kingdom, it was necessary to keep the gods satisfied.

View into the roofed hall of columns

03

THE PARTHENON

When visiting Athens in 1911, the architect Le Corbusier stated that "the Parthenon, this terrible machine, turns everything within a radius of three miles to dust." This impressive marble temple on the Acropolis above Athens took no notice – it's still regarded as the epitome of Greek architecture and ancient culture, and one of the key works of Western architecture.

The Parthenon, Athens, Greece
447–432 BC

CHRONOLOGY

In the 5th century BC, Athens – and with it the surrounding region of Attica – developed into one of the largest and most powerful city-states in ancient Greece. Athens often found itself in mortal conflict with the Persians but, in the decades between 450 and 400 BC, the situation greatly improved. Athens flourished under the leadership of a charismatic leader, Pericles: the city became an important commercial centre with a wide-spread network of trading connections, and secured its influence with a large navy. And as the city-state evolved, so did its culture.

A Home for the City's Goddess

Building projects also flourished during this period. Pericles began the construction of the temple on the Acropolis (Greek for "upper-city"), which had been destroyed by the Persians. The Parthenon Temple was the major building of the prestigious project. This huge temple, built entirely of white marble, was much larger than the previous building, and yet was erected in a mere 15 years. The western front of the richly decorated building was adorned with eight Doric columns, and there were 17 columns on each of the long sides. Construction of the Parthenon, following plans by the architect Iktinos, was completed around 432 BC. It resisted the ravages of time until the late 17th century, when a shot from a Venetian cannon hit the Turkish gunpowder store in the Parthenon and destroyed a major section of the building.

The Parthenon was dedicated to the patron goddess of the city, Athena, but was not reserved solely for her. It was even more important as a place for storing the state's treasures. Through this impressive city memorial, temple and treasure house, Athens proclaimed its wealth and power. The sculptural decoration was correspondingly lavish: Pericles commissioned the sculptor Phidias, who was already famous, to carve the temple's decoration. This consisted of the sculptures on the triangular pediments at the ends of the temple, and a 160-metre (525-foot) relief frieze featuring depictions of battles, which ran around the building.

Criticism and Exile

Despite the success of the project, both Pericles and Phidias received severe criticism. Pericles was accused by his Athenian contemporaries of misusing their money for city beautification – the constructions costs amounted to five tons of silver! He was able to save himself by drawing attention to the positive results of the undertaking: above all, he had created many jobs and encouraged a revival in the arts and crafts. Phidias, however, did not get off as easily. He was accused by his co-workers of having embezzled large sums of money when he created the 12-metre (40-foot) high bronze statue of Athena, and he was finally forced to go into exile.

The most famous surviving building of ancient Greece: the Parthenon

04 PETRA

More than 80 percent of Jordan is covered by stone and lava deserts, the rest by sand. So it's astonishing, in the midst of the stones in the south-west of the country, to find the remains of an ancient city. Petra was the main settlement – and later royal city – of the desert people the Nabataeans.

Petra, Jordan
Constructed 100 BC–AD 200

The city in stone was already a popular travel destination when the American film director Steven Spielberg made it known to a much wider audience. The Sik, the narrow gorge leading into the city, was the location for the final part of his Indiana Jones trilogy. In *Indiana Jones and the Last Crusade*, the star of the film, Harrison Ford, is involved in the search for the Holy Grail. The impressive façade of the Khazne Firaun – the "Pharaoh's Treasury" – served as the background for the film's showdown.

The culture of the Nabataeans reached its peak around 2,000 years ago. Mainly traders who constantly travelled long distances, originally the Nabataeans did not live in a precisely defiled region, and only gradually settled in towns and villages along the Incense Road, which linked Egypt with north Arabia and India. Petra was a junction of two important desert routes. A modest trading post rapidly developed into a commercial and political centre, and the growing affluence of the city was accompanied by major building projects.

A City in the Desert

At the time of the Nabataeans, the Sik – a long, narrow and rocky gorge almost 70 metres (230 feet) high – was the main route into the city area of Petra. Once visitors had passed through the Sik, they found themselves facing an entire city literally carved out of solid sandstone. At the height of its success, approximately 10,000 people lived in this rocky desert city, whose stones shimmer in a multitude of colours from pink, shades of yellow and white, to light grey. So far, archaeologists have explored only one percent of the city area of Petra, even though the scientific investigation of the trading centre began in the early 19th century. Since then, many public buildings – including a theatre for around 8,000 spectators – have been unearthed. Excavation still continues to bring new wonders to light.

Building for a Life after Death

The deep valley of Petra is strewn with monumental tombs and orderly rows of much smaller tombs. The façades of some of the grave chambers are several metres high and occasionally span two storeys. The size and sculptural decoration of the tombs vary; some of the simpler ones are framed by flat columns, others are adorned with obelisks. To create these monuments, masons had first to create a flat surface on the stone, and then carve more three-dimensional forms, such as columns and pediments, merlons and arches. Occasionally the façades of the tombs were decorated with plaster or coloured.

The Khazne Firaun – the "Pharaoh's Treasury" – displays the most famous façade of the city. This large building, enclosed by solid rock, was probably not a treasure house, but very little is known about its actual function, or even when it was built. The two-storey façade of the red-sandstone building rises to a height of 40 metres (131 feet). The central four of the six columns on the lower floor support a large pediment, above which there stands a round, pavilion-like structure that rises up between a large broken pediment on the upper floor. Stone sarcophagi were probably placed in the chambers in the interior of this so-called treasure house, though there is still a great deal of debate over whether the Khazne Firaun was actually a storehouse, temple or tomb.

The Khazne Firaun, the Pharaoh's Treasury

05

THE COLOSSEUM

"Pecunia non olet – money doesn't smell" is a saying attributed to the builder of the Colosseum, Emperor Vespasian. And actually the "latrine tax" he introduced was not a bad source of income. In any case, the Emperor didn't have to worry about money when undertaking this mammoth building project, as can be seen from the time it took to complete it – work began in AD 72, and the huge stadium was ready a mere eight years later.

The Colosseum, Rome, Italy
72–80 AD

FACT FILE
Materials
  Brick, travertine and concrete
Total height
  48.5 m/159 ft
Area
  Approx. 19,000 sq m/204,510 sq ft
Greatest expanse
  188 x 156 m/617 x 512 ft
Capacity
  Approx. 50,000–70,000 spectators
Use until 5th C AD
  Amphitheatre

Four floors rise almost 50 metres (164 feet) above the elliptical ground plan, whose greatest expanse measures a stately 188 x 156 metres (617 x 512 feet). The floors are divided into galleries and sections, and a sophisticated system of passages and entrances assured that the events, which attracted thousands of spectators, went off without a hitch. When the amphitheatre was opened, the Romans were able to enjoy a hundred days of games, all of which were free, a gift of the emperor. Fights between gladiators and animal were very popular, and the arena could even be flooded for the enactment of naval battles.

From Stadium to Stone Quarry
The last games probably took place in AD 523, and for centuries nothing much was heard of the arena to the west of the Forum Romanum. However, the mania of the Renaissance popes for grand building projects once again drew attention to Rome's ancient ruins. In fact, many of the Church Fathers had used them to supply building materials for their churches and palaces. The Colosseum was a rich source, providing not only travertine stone, but also, in particular, concrete and bricks, as well as marble, which had been used to face the lower rows of seats. Even the lead clamps that had been used to secure one stone block to the next were much sought-after by later builders. And the Colosseum was ravaged not only by the builders of the early period of modern history: it was also severely damaged by fires and earthquakes. Yet in spite of all this, around two-fifths of the building has survived.

Column Orders
From the outside, the galleries of the Colosseum are accentuated by vertical axes – arches and columns that could be straight out of the chapter on "column orders" in a Roman's "architect's handbook." In Classical architecture there are several column types, categorised according to the style of their base, shaft and (above all) capital. Plain Doric columns are found on the lower floors of the Colosseum. Ionic columns, which have more elaborate capitals, grace the second floor. The columns used for the third floor supposedly originated in the wealthy commercial centre of Corinth: the richly decorated Corinthian capital is similar to the Ionian, though with the addition of leaves and other plant motifs. Emperor Vespasian didn't survive to see the completion of the fourth floor – his son and successor, Domitian, added this after his father's death. This was not merely for aesthetic reasons: awnings to protect the crowd from the fierce sun could be attached above the small window openings. Some of the 50,000 to 70,000 spectators obviously preferred a seat in the shade.

Site of gladiator battles: the Colosseum in Rome

06

TIKAL

The remains of the ancient Maya city of Tikal lie in the midst of the rainforests of the province of El Petén in the north of Guatemala. In the 5th century BC, the Tikal civilization covered an area of almost 64 square kilometres (25 square miles).

Tikal, Guatemala
2nd–9th C AD

CHRONOLOGY

ca. 600 BC	Settlements in the Tikal area
AD 378	Tikal becomes an important centre in the El Petén region
682–723	Reign of King Ah Cacao (Prince Chocolate)
ca. 800	Tikal has a population of between 80,000 and 100,000
879	Last record of the city being inhabited
1881/82	Systematic study of Tikal begins under the direction of Hiram Bingham
1950–61	Extensive excavations undertaken
Since 1955	National Park
1979	UNESCO World Heritage Site

Research into Tikal began in the 19th century, when the site was overgrown with dense vegetation. Temples and palaces were gradually uncovered and made accessible to the public, and now Tikal is regarded as one of the best researched Maya cities, with the power to attract both tourists and scholars.

Thriving Community

The area was already settled in the 7th century BC, but Tikal experienced its high point in the 5th century AD. More than 3,000 individual buildings, including palace complexes, squares and street, steles and water reservoirs, as well as simple living quarters, have been identified in the central area of the city, which was protected by substantial defence fortifications. At the peak of the city's development, around 75,000 persons lived in an area of approximately 15 square kilometres (six square miles). At that time, magnificent buildings were erected, together with hundreds of stone steles that record the history of the city and the deeds of its most prominent citizens. In addition, the highest temple pyramid in Mesoamerica – Temple IV, which is almost 56 metres (184 feet) high – is located in the west of Tikal.

The political heart, however, was in its centre, on the Great Plaza, which was lined with altars and temples. The ruler Hasaw Kan K'awil rests under a nine-stepped pyramid, Temple I, the Temple of the Great Jaguar, on the east side of the square. Temple II, the Mood Temple, erected on a three-tiered base, stands opposite. Both were plastered white originally, while their distinctive roof "combs" were decorated in bright colours. The largest ensemble of buildings in Tikal can be found to the north of this main square. This is the North Acropolis, which has a building history covering around 1,000 years. Temples and tombs were erected on various levels and could be reached by steep flights of stone steps. The rulers spread themselves out over the south-east of the Great Plaza; their labyrinthine palace complex stretched over several inner courtyards and the numerous rooms of the palace were connected to each other by underground corridors. And of course Tikal, like other Mesoamerican sites, did not lack a field for ritual ballgames.

The End of a Civilization

Researchers have been successful in decoding the Maya's hieroglyphic script, and now more and more is known of the achievements of this advanced civilization, which had an extremely well-developed calendar, and whose kings included Smoke Frog, Great Jaguar Paw and Prince Chocolate. This research also made the reasons for Tikal's decline and fall much clearer. In AD 509, King Chak Tok Ich'aak II was taken prisoner and died without leaving a successor. In 562, Tikal's arch-enemy, Calakmul, conquered the city. It appears that most of the population then emigrated. By the 9th century AD, the city was completely deserted.

The Jaguar Temple in the Maya city of Tikal

07

HAGIA SOPHIA

At the time of its construction, Hagia Sophia, the Church of the Holy Wisdom, was regarded as the eighth wonder of the world. For centuries, Hagia Sophia, in the heart of the cultural and commercial centre of Constantinople (today Istanbul), was by far the largest church in the Christian world.

Hagia Sophia, Istanbul, Turkey
AD 532–537

FACT FILE
Builder Emperor Justinian I
Architects Anthemios of Tralles and
   Isidoros of Milet
Area Approx. 70 x 75 m/230 x 246 ft
Wall-surface area More than 10,000
   sq m/107,640 sq ft
Height of dome Almost 56 m/184 ft
Costs Approx. 145 tons of gold
Use Originally a church, then a
   mosque and, since 1934, a museum

Generations of scholars have pondered over how it was possible for 6th-century builders to construct a free-floating dome almost 56 metres (183 feet) high and 31 metres (102 feet) wide. None of the plans for the impressive domed roof, which rests on only four massive pillars, has come down to us. However, its architects are known: Anthemios of Tralles and the mathematician Isidoros of Milet were the men commissioned by Emperor Justinian I to build a new cathedral in the capital of the Eastern Roman Empire. Hagia Sophia, constructed in the mere five years between 532 and 537, unified the needs of religion (it was primarily a bishop's church) with those of the court and the state. Justinian invested the staggering amount of 145 tons of gold in the construction of the building, and – if one can believe the historian Procopios – was even actively involved in the planning and building, personally visiting the site every day to reassure himself that progress was being made.

Collapse
However, one year after the church's consecration, the dome collapsed – it had not survived for very long in an area where earthquakes are frequent. The downward thrust of the first dome caused the pillars and supporting arches to bend and they were forced outwards. The nephew of Isidoros of Milet immediately began the reconstruction: he increased the height of the buttresses, moved some of the columns, and rebuilt the walls. And, after all these changes had been implemented, the building was topped with an even higher dome, and consecrated at Christmas 562. And – if we overlook a few major and minor repairs – it has stood firm to this day.

From Church to Mosque
The design combines two basic forms of church: a "directional" basilica and a centrally planed building. The central space is dominated by the main dome, with smaller domes on the west and east. The domes, side aisles and galleries cover an area of 10,000 square metres (107,640 square feet) and were originally decorated with mosaics on a gold ground, and with sheets of white marble. Some remnants of these can still be seen. Little of the decoration of the Christian church has been preserved, however, for after the conquest of Constantinople by Sultan Mehmet II, Hagia Sophia became the main mosque of the Ottoman Empire. Christian symbols were replaced by Moslem ones, the icons were removed, and the mosaics inside the church were hidden or plastered over because of the Islamic ban on figurative images. Four minarets were constructed, and these still dominate the external appearance of this unique building, which now serves as a museum.

The interior of the Hagia Sophia: built as a Christian church, transformed into a mosque and used today as a museum

It is regarded as the most important Byzantine construction: the Hagia Sophia

08

SAN VITALE

Constantinople (today Istanbul in Turkey) had developed into an important cultural centre following the division of the Roman Empire. In the 6th century AD, Emperor Justinian pushed forward with his plans to expand the East Roman Empire, and the Byzantines conquered the small northern Italian city of Ravenna in 526. They stayed 200 years, and clearly left their mark.

San Vitale, Ravenna, Italy
AD 526–547

CHARACTERISTICS
Diameter of the dome 16 m / 53 ft
Consecration April 19, 548
Addition to the UNESCO World Heritage List 1996

In AD 526, Emperor Justinian laid the foundation stone for the Church of San Vitale. The building has an octagonal central section in front of which there's a vestibule. The dome, also octagonal, and with a diameter of 16 metres (52 feet), forms a vault over the central room. The central area is surrounded by an ambulatory, with light flowing in through round-arched windows. The ambulatory rises over two storeys; galleries vaulted over by half-domes are located on the upper storey, and both storeys open to the interior through high Norman arches. The external appearance of the church, which was completed in 547, is dominated by simple brickwork, and the dome is covered by a modest roof in the form of a low, many-sided pyramid. The interior of San Vitale, however, is a different story.

Glorious Mosaics

The mosaic decoration of the central building begins immediately above the high marble base. The adornment on the walls of San Vitale is one of the few surviving examples of Byzantine mosaic art dating from late antiquity. The greater portion of the decoration of the churches fell victim to the iconoclasts of the 8th and 9th centuries, who destroyed religious images considered to be impious.

However, the pictorial programme in San Vitale is still easy to interpret. Scenes from the New and Old Testaments face each other. Above the window area of the back wall, we see Christ enthroned between saints and archangels. In the semi-circular end of the altar room, the apse, the mosaics are particularly impressive. These images, which also adorn the vaulted ceiling, appear to be covered with a golden shimmer.

The walls are peopled with angels and saints, and the alcoves and walls are decorated with architectural depictions and vegetal and geometric ornamentation. Countless tesserae – small cubes of coloured glass or stone used in mosaic – contribute to the glorious impression created by the interior, which is further enhanced by the light falling through the high windows.

Emperor Charlemagne seems to have been less impressed by the magnificent decoration than by the octagonal form, and was greatly inspired by this Italian church when constructing his chapel in Aachen around AD 800 (see pages 32–34).

The apse with the Enthroned Christ

HORYUJI TEMPLE

Created at the beginning of the 7th century AD, the Horyuji is the oldest Buddhist temple complex in Japan. It is also the only completely preserved sacred building from the early period of Buddhist architecture.

Horyuji Temple, Nara, Japan
Start of construction, 7th C AD

The history of the Horyuji Temple dates back to a vow of Emperor Yōmei.
Out of thanks for his recovery from illness, Yōmei had promised to erect a temple and statue of Buddha. He died, however, before he could put his plan into action. The crown prince Shōtoku and Empress Suiko fulfilled Yōmei's last wish and began to build the temple. In 1993, the Temple site became the first Japanese monument to be added to the UNESCO World Heritage List.

Buddhism made its way to Japan from China and Korea in the middle of the 6th century AD. The Japanese court regarded the new religion as an opportunity for uniting the country and for strengthening their own power; major construction works soon followed. The impressive temple complexes that resulted had a new and distinctive architectural form: they were built around a hall placed on a platform with its supports and the roof resting on wooden columns.

A Buddhist Prince

The Horyuji Temple, located 10 kilometres (6 miles) south-west of Nara in the south of the main island of Japan, is a product of this early stage of Buddhist architecture. Prince Shotoku, a declared admirer of Buddhism, had work on the temple started in the year 607. Under his rule, many Korean labourers went to Japan to construct and decorate the numerous temples. Shotoku paid particular attention to two complexes: the Shitennoji Temple, in what is today Osaka, and his first building project, Horyuji.

The temple area at Horyuji is surrounded by a wall. In the west, a two-tiered gate leads into the interior. The most important of the 31 buildings in the complex are located in the western section of the temple. The eastern temple sector was erected in the 8th century and consists of 14 buildings. The heart of this smaller complex is the octagonal Yumedono, the Hall of Dreams, where the body of the princely founder of the temple rests.

A Masterpiece in Wood

The main building in the western section, the Kodo, or Golden Hall, which consists of two storeys built over a rectangular plan, is the oldest wooden building in the world. The posts that support the massive roof are painted a reddish-brown, while the walls in between are plastered white. The heart of the building is a richly decorated room – called the *moya* – containing an altar and shrines. The verandas, the *hisashi,* which lead around this central room, are covered by a protruding roof.

After a fire had destroyed large sections of the building in 670, it was reconstructed in the original style using cypress wood. At that time, the pagoda was moved and, since then, has been located to the left of the Golden Hall, which disturbs the symmetry of the original plan. The five-tiered pagoda is also ancient; in fact it's the oldest in Japan. A reading room in the north closes the inner area of the temple. Over the centuries, additional buildings, including two modern treasuries, have found their way into the Horyuji ensemble.

Architecture from the early years of Buddhism: The Horyuji Temple complex

PALATINE CHAPEL IN AACHEN

One of the major building complexes of the Middle Ages, the palace complex at Aachen in Germany provided all that an emperor needed: fortified living accommodation, storerooms, fine reception areas and a chapel. The emperor didn't have permanent residence, so he had to move continuously throughout his large kingdom. His various palaces served not only practical needs: they were a direct and very visible expression of his power.

Palatine Chapel, Aachen, Germany
ca. 790–800

Under Charles the Great (748–848), art, literature and architecture experienced a boom, and the period in which he reigned is called the Carolingian Renaissance. Under his government, the cloisters St Gallen, Reichenau and Tegernsee became considerably more important. In 1978, the Aachen Cathedral and the Palatine Chapel became the first German monuments to be added to the UNESCO World Heritage List.

Most of the buildings at Aachen are known only from excavations. In fact, only one building has survived intact – but this, fortunately, is its remarkable chapel. Aachen was located in the east of Emperor Charlemagne's realm, and his decision to erect his most important palace at this seemingly insignificant location may be connected with the warm thermal springs there, which had already been appreciated by the Romans.

The Chapel and Imperial Power

Construction of the imperial palace began just after 790. Extensive outbuildings, which guaranteed that provisions were available for the travelling court, were part of the living complexes, as was a fine reception room.

The chapel is entered by an impressive portal on its western side. The main domed room is a two-storey octagon with a diameter of almost 20 metres (65 feet). A large choir is attached on the east side. Arches open the octagon to the vaulted 16-sided ambulatory. Galleries are located on the upper floor behind arches supported by tall, slender columns. Some of the columns and capitals in the upper church are *spolia*, in other words material taken from ancient ruins. Charlemagne was not satisfied with just any old pieces; he had selected treasures delivered to him from Ravenna in Italy (see pages 28–29). This was the Emperor's way of creating a direct link with the magnificent buildings of the last capital city of the West Roman Empire. He had obtained the Pope's personal permission to carry off columns from the palace in Ravenna to Aachen. Set very visibly in the Aachen chapel, these *spolia* stress the importance of the church in which Charlemagne's throne stood.

From Chapel to Cathedral

Odo von Metz has been identified as the architect of the chapel at Aachen, but that is all that is known about him. The building was consecrated in 805 by an illustrious person – Pope Leo III himself travelled all the way from Rome to the remote town for this very purpose. Nine years later, Emperor Charlemagne was buried there.

For more than 200 years, Charlemagne's chapel was the tallest building north of the Alps. A lot has happened to it since then, and today the octagon forms the centre of Aachen Cathedral. A Gothic choir and chapels were added, and the interior decoration changed. At the end of the 18th century, Napoleon had the ancient spolia columns removed to Paris. However, with the exception of four that are still in the Louvre, they have since been returned to Aachen.

It forms the centre of the Aachen Minster: Charlemagne's Palatine Chapel

The *cathedra* regalis: The kings were crowned on this simple marble throne

The interior of the octagon with the low ambulatory and gallery

11

BOROBUDUR

Monastery, burial place or simply a symbol of power? Borobudur's real function is still a matter of dispute. However, there is a general consensus that this temple, in the centre of the Indonesian island of Java, represents a Buddhist meditation image (mandala) of colossal size.

Borobudur, Java, Indonesia
ca. 800

The significance of the name Borobudur cannot be clearly defined. It most likely refers to a combination of the terms *bara* and *budur*. *Bara* could come from *Vihara*, a Javanese designation for a complex of temples or cloisters.

The work involved was enormous. Labourers fitted together two million stone blocks to form a vast pyramid without leaving the slightest space between them. The seven-tiered temple rises above a square base, the side of which measure 113 metres (370 feet). The lower zone is formed by four square galleries, the upper zone by three round terraces, all constructed of unplastered stone. The stairs and step-like gates connect the different levels. The three concentric circles support a total of 72 stupas, each of them with a seated figure of the Buddha, with the large central stupa crowning the highest tier.

Sleeping for a Thousand Years

The Borobudur temple was built around AD 800, during the reign of the Shailendra kings. Their period of rule over central Java is impressively recorded by the remarkable Borobudur temple, which was reached by a pilgrimage route lined with other temples. The Candi Pawon and Candi Menut complexes, located in the immediate vicinity of the mother temple, are considerably smaller but just as richly decorated with reliefs. Despite its overwhelming size, Borobudur soon fell into oblivion, and was uncovered from beneath the tropical vegetation only at the beginning of the 19th century. Sadly, its rediscovery meant that it was soon being looted for stone and art treasures. For this reason, extravagant security measures were implemented in the 1970s. And in order to ensure its structural safety, the entire temple was dismantled, the earth beneath it stabilized, and Borobudur painstakingly rebuilt.

Journey to Enlightenment

Since then, the oversized mandala has once again greeted thousands of visitors. In the Buddhist religion, mandalas are designs, made up largely of overlapping squares and circles, representing the spiritual universe. Borobudur depicts this map of this universe precisely, its squares and circles represent different stages in the journey to Enlightenment. Numerous pilgrims still visit Borobudur each day, and if they pace around the terraces of the building in a clockwise direction they may find their way to Nirvana, the final stage of enlightenment.

Their journey is graphically illustrated in the many stories depicted on the stone reliefs – 2.5 kilometres (1.5 miles) of them in all – which decorate the inner walls of the gallery-like ambulatory. The life of the historic Buddha is depicted on the lower level, together with scenes from the everyday life in 8th- and 9th-century Java. Higher up, the chaos of human existence is left behind and pilgrims enter the realm of eternal bliss. The pictorial programme here consists of around 1,500 scenes. After this picture book in stone, it is not only Nirvana that awaits visitors – but also the throng of tourists in the archaeological park at the foot of the temple!

Aerial view of Borobudur

THE MEZQUITA

Under Islamic rule, the Iberian Peninsula experienced a cultural flowering in the fields of art and architecture that lasted well into the 11th century. The Mezquita, the Grand Mosque, in Córdoba – one of the largest Islamic sacred buildings in the world – was erected in just one year.

Mezquita, Córdoba, Spain
From AD 785

FACT FILE
Construction time Approx. 900 years (with interruptions)
Length 175 m/574 ft
Width 128 m/420 ft
Total area 24,000 sq m/258,334 sq ft
Number of chapels More than 50
Number of columns More than 1,000
Function Since 1236, Catholic church

The interior of the Mezquita has more than 1,000 individual pillars, made out of granite, marble, onyx and jasper. The structure, along with the historic centre of Córdoba, was added to the UNESCO World Heritage List in 1984.

Andalusia had seen a broad range of building projects under Islamic rule. In the 10th century, there were over half a million inhabitants in Córdoba alone, which had more than 300 mosques, the same number of public baths, 50 hospitals, 80 public schools, 20 libraries and 17 universities. The Mezquita rises above the centre of the old city of Córdoba, overlooking the River Guadalquivir. It resembles a fortress: its high sandstone walls are crowned with battlements and buttresses, the whole building being set on a large rectangular base measuring 175 metres (575 feet) in length and 128 metres (420 feet) in breadth.

In the Forest of Columns
The main entrance to the mosque, the Puerta del Pérdon, is on the northern side next to the bell tower where, originally, a minaret stood. Fountains for the ritual ablutions of the faithful were located in the Orange Courtyard, which is surrounded by arcades. Countless arcades run through the interior of the mosque. Their horseshoe-shaped arches are two-toned (made of red brick and light sandstone) and rest on simple columns. Under Abd ar-Rahman I, the Mezquita already had 11 naves with 12 vaulted bays. His successors continued with construction until the building ultimately reached a size many times greater than that of the original. In the 16th century, an enormous cathedral was built in the centre of the former mosque, which had to sacrifice four rows of arches.

Lavish Decoration
The prayer alcove, the *mihrab*, on the south wall of the Mezquita is especially magnificent. Al-Hakam II, who speeded up the extension of the mosque around 960, paid personal attention to this. He asked the Byzantine Emperor to send him a mosaic artist to instruct the local crafts-men in this technique. He came – and brought with him the 16 tons of stone material necessary for framing the octagonal prayer alcove. Since then, mosaics in an unending array of colours have glittered upon the golden ground. The most important element in the *mihrab*, as in Islamic art in general, is calligraphy. The depiction of God is forbidden in Islam and so ornaments and written characters are important forms of decorative expression. Arabic calligraphy is a major ornamental motif not only in architecture, but also in ceramics, metal work and textiles.

Columns inside the Mezquita

next pages: The Mezquita, built as a mosque is, today, the Cathedral of Córdoba

THE HRADČANY

Construction of the Hradčany, high above the River Vltava in Prague, began as early as the end of the 9th century AD. It served as an easily defended palace for the country's princes: a castle eventually surrounded by a ring wall. It grew with each successive generation, and soon the Bishop of Prague joined the princes. Since 1918, the castle over the Vltava has also been the official residence of the President of the Czech Republic.

Hradčany, Prague, Czech Republic
Beginning of construction 9th C AD

Peter Parler
The main cathedral architect Peter Parler came from Schwäbisch Gmünd, but lived primarily in Prague after the middle of the 14th century. He spent his period of training in the Cologne Domhütte and, along with other members of the Parler family, he was responsible for the construction of the Holy Cross Church of Münster in Schwäbisch Gmünd until he took over the construction of St Vitus.

Over the centuries, many very different builders left their traces on the Hradčany, so that late Gothic vaults can be admired along with Baroque and Neo-Classical features. The sturdy castle walls shield three inner courtyards. The first, located at the entrance to Hradčany Square, was created in the middle of the 18th century and is the most recent. The second, situated behind the imposing Matthias Gate, was built during the Renaissance and the Baroque and clearly reflects their architectural styles.

Gothic Origins

Initially, life in the castle was confined mainly to the third courtyard. The most magnificent building in the Hradčany, St Vitus Cathedral, stands on its northern side. In 1344, shortly after Pope Clement VI had declared Prague an Episcopal See, the cornerstone for a Gothic cathedral of impressive dimensions was laid. The French architect Matthias of Arras was responsible for planning a choir that is 47 metres (154 feet) long and almost 40 metres (130 feet) high. After his death, the master builder Peter Parler, who was only 23 years old at the time, was commissioned to continue the construction. Parler, and later his sons, not only completed the choir and introduced a new system of vaulting, but also immortalized themselves in the church's interior: along with the royal family, the stone busts of the builders look down on the visitors from between the arcades and windows. However, not even the Parlers were able to complete the Prague Cathedral – this did not occur until the beginning of the 20th century.

A Fall and its Consequences

The royal palace, which is located on the east side of the third and oldest courtyard, acted as the seat of the sovereign until the 16th century. It too has a very complicated building history, for each ruler undertook extensions and renovations. In the 15th century, the Riders' Staircase was built for the participants of tournaments: it made it possible for the knights to ride directly into the Vladislav Hall. The 62-metre (200-foot) long room on the second floor of the building is made elegant by its extraordinary vaulting.

One room in the south-east of the palace complex is more infamous than famous. In 1618, the imperial governors and their secretaries were thrown out of a window of the small room into the moat. Despite falling 15 metres (50 feet), they survived. However, the political consequences of the revolution were grave: this second "Defenestration of Prague" (there had been an earlier one in 1419) led to the Bohemian uprising against the Habsburg emperor and so, ultimately, to the catastrophic Thirty Years' War.

The Vladislav Hall where tournaments and festivities took place

next pages: View of the Hradčany

14

DURHAM CATHEDRAL

The Benedictine abbey in the small town of Durham in the north of England has monks from the nearby island of Lindisfarne to thank for its foundation. Fearing attacks from the Vikings, they left their island monastery in the 10th century and sought a suitable resting place for the remains of their illustrious predecessor, St Cuthbert.

CHRONOLOGY

Before 1133 Choir, nave and transept built
ca. 1100 Choir vaulted
1170–75 Galilee Chapel in the west of the cathedral added
13th C East transept built
1217–26 West tower front built
1242–80 Nine-altar chapel in the east of the cathedral added
1465–90 Transept tower rebuilt after being struck by lightning
1650 Becomes a camp for Scottish prisoners of war
1986 UNESCO World Heritage Site

After long years of searching, they were finally successful. To this very day, the relics of the bishop rest in Durham cathedral, which stands on a cliff overlooking the city centre and the River Wear. There, on the impressive site at the highest point of Durham, work on the monumental cathedral was begun in 1093. The cathedral that was built reflects both the power of the Bishops of Durham, and also the popularity of the St Cuthbert, who attracted huge numbers of pilgrims.

Saints or Sinners

This Romanesque basilica, which is 143 metres (470 feet) long, is characterized by mighty walls and massive round arches. The impressive west front is dominated by two towers, and a huge tower rises over the crossing, where the nave and transepts meet. The grave of St Cuthbert is located in the choir at the eastern end of the cathedral. The cathedral became very popular, and it was not only the numerous pilgrims who were able to count on a friendly welcome: any criminal who reached the bronze lion's-head door opener on the north-west portal could rely on being granted asylum – even murderers.

Romanesque and Gothic

The impression created by the interior is one of power and size. Monumental pillars, with a circumference of up to six metres (20 feet), support the powerful round arches of the lower section. These columns are decorated with a variety of patterns, including the zigzag forms typical of Norman design. Knowledge of the technology needed to build large-scale churches had come to England in the wake of the Norman conquest in 1066. Following the invasion, the Norman style of building (Romanesque) became widespread in England.

However, the builders of Durham Cathedral didn't simply take on a well-known architectural art form: they made their own advances, some of which anticipated the Gothic style. This is seen above all in its vaulted choir, where work began around 1100 and took 30 years to complete. The design was novel: here the weight is carried not by heavy, round arches but by vaults in which thin ribs form a framework that becomes the load-bearing structure. The spaces in between the ribs are lightly filled. The lightness and elegance of this form of structure, which is known as ribbed vaulting, forms a strong contrast to the massive Romanesque forms in the rest of the cathedral. It was here, in Durham Cathedral, that ribbed vaulting, which would be important in the development of Gothic structures, was first used successfully.

Monumental columns with zigzag patterns in the interior

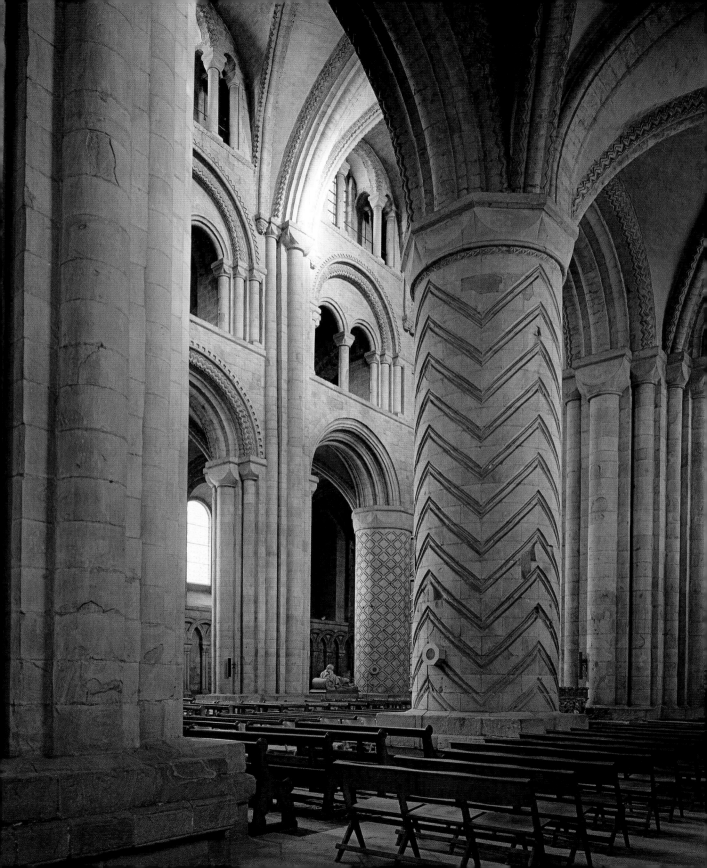

15

ANGKOR WAT

The world's largest temple complex was hidden under tropical vegetation for centuries. It was not until the 19th century that this masterpiece of the Khmer Empire, buried beneath tree roots and luxuriant foliage, once again saw the light of day. With its hundreds of small temples, pools, canals and rich sculptural decoration, Cambodia's most famous sacred building is undoubtedly one of the wonders of world architecture.

Angkor Wat, Cambodia
Beginning of construction 12th C

FACT FILE
Area 1,300 x 1,500 m / 4,260 x 4,920 ft
Sculptural decoration Reliefs cover more than 1,000 sq m / 10,760 sq ft
Use Temple

Maps of the location of the individual temples, as well as information on the construction and historical background, can be found at: http://theangkorguide.com/

In the 9th century AD, the Khmer, the people living in what is now Cambodia, increased in importance and power in South-East Asia. Ultimately, their empire extended far beyond the borders of present-day Cambodia to incorporate parts of Vietnam and Thailand, reaching its peak between the 11th and 13th centuries. Trading boomed, waterways were cut, and a sophisticated irrigation programme made rice farming the economic basis for the population. To reflect this affluence and power, work began on an enormous temple complex, Angkor Wat (or Vat).

A Temple City is Born
It was probably during the reign of King Surayavarman I in the first half of the 12th century AD that the Khmer began the construction of Angkor Wat, which is situated between the great lakes and Mount Kulen, to the south of the old capital, Angkor Thom. Angkor means "main city", a fact reflected in the dimensions the project assumed during the 37 years of its construction. Thousands of labourers, stonemasons, landscape designers, sculptors and architects planned and built the complex out of sandstone, surrounding the site with moats used for both transport and irrigation. Today, not one name is known from the multitude of men who built the complex, which measures 1,300 x 1,500 metres (4,260 x 4,920 feet).

The principal axis of Angkor Wat runs from west to east, with the main gate being located in the west. The central temple tower rises above a base of 365 x 250 metres (1,179 x 820 feet) and its three tiers reach a height of 65 metres (214 feet). Four additional towers surround it.

The Seat of the Gods
The walls encircling Angkor Wat, along which processions once made their way, are richly decorated with stone reliefs. These depict mythological and historical scenes from Hinduism and Buddhism, wars, victories over demons, scenes in heaven and hell. This mythology is not restricted to these external walls: the entire Angkor Wat complex is a representation of the Hindu concept of the cosmos. The world is shown as a square surrounded by mountains (walls and temples) and infinite oceans (pools). The rich symbolism of the site, both in its very structure and in its many images, has given rise to endless debate and speculation. In terms of overall function, it's clear that Angkor Wat was consecrated to the god Vishnu and the god-king Jayavarman II. It is also beyond doubt that this temple complex is a tribute to the sophisticated engineering and artistic skills of the Khmer.

The towers of Angkor Wat are in the form of lotus buds

next pages: The silhouette of the temple mountain of Angkor Wat; in keeping with Hindu beliefs, it represents the blueprint of the cosmos

16

NOTRE-DAME

Many older churches had to be demolished to make space for the construction of the bishop's church on the island in the Seine in Paris. After all, it was intended that in size and splendour this cathedral should surpass all the other cathedrals of France.

Notre-Dame, Paris, France
From 1163

CHRONOLOGY

1163	Foundation stone laid
1177	Choir built
ca. 1200	West front completed
1240	South tower built
1250	North tower and Kings' Gallery added
13th C	Transept fronts completed
1792	Damaged extensively during the French Revolution
1843	Reconstruction begins under the direction of the architects Lassus and Viollet-le-Duc
2019	During restoration work, the roof caught fire and burned for some 15 hours, damaging the central lead-clad wooden spire

On Quasimodo's tracks: the cathedral is the scene of Victor Hugo's historical novel *Notre-Dame de Paris* (1831, The Hunchback of Notre-Dame), which has also become famous through numerous films. The deformed bell-ringer Quasimodo observed life on the streets of medieval Paris from the top of the church's towers.

The King himself donated 200 livres for the new building: the cathedral would greatly increase his prestige, and he would be able to see it from his palace. However, the sum was in no way sufficient for such an ambitious project, and the man who had ordered work to begin, Bishop Maurice de Sully, had to finance the lion's share from his own coffers. Well, that's what his successor claimed. No matter how this major project was actually financed, construction began in 1163 and Notre-Dame was completed about 50 years later. The dimensions were huge for the time: the building is over 130 metres (426 feet) long, and the nave is 35 metres (115 feet) high. The west front, which was begun around 1200, is lavishly ornamented with sculptures: above the three richly decorated portals leading into the interior there is a horizontal gallery with 28 carved figures of kings, each separated from the next by a column. Above this gallery, there is a large round window. Two square towers flank the central section and are connected to each other by a series of tall, pointed arches.

The Light of God

In the 13th century, the end walls of the transepts were decorated with large rose windows; the finely decorated window on the north transept has a diameter of 13 metres (43 feet). Light is the key: the symbolism of light plays an important role not only in this cathedral, but in all Gothic cathedrals. The abbot of the St Denis Monastery to the north of Paris argued that a church should be an image of the Temple of Solomon, as described in the biblical Book of Wisdom. In this sense, the believer entering the west portal of a church could be seen as passing through the gates of Heaven into the light of God. In order to make the best use of light, large windows were necessary, and this meant piercing the thick wall. The development of buttresses was essential in this process, for the use of external buttresses to support a building meant that it was no longer necessary for the external walls to bear the weight of the vaults and the roof. As the walls no longer had this key structural role, they could be opened up to create larger and larger windows, with the huge expanses of glass being supported by a framework of stone tracery. These windows not only allowed light to flood into the interior, they also provided an area in which biblical stories could be illustrated.

The choir of Notre-Dame

next pages: Towers on west façade

17

CASTEL DEL MONTE

To this day, it is still not known if its builder, Emperor Frederick II, ever actually set foot in the Castel del Monte. However, this castle in southern Italy certainly meant a lot to him, and it's reported that he was even involved in its design.

Castel del Monte, Andria, Italy
ca. 1240

CHARACTERISTICS

Height of the main octagon
25 m/82 ft
Height of the tower
26 m/85 ft
Length of the side of the octagon
16.5 m/54 ft
Length of the sides of the tower
3.1 m/10 ft

Castel del Monte was added to the UNESCO World Heritage List in 1996.

The castle, which is now shrouded in mystery, lies on a hilltop in the barren landscape of Apulia, 16 kilometres (10 miles) from the Adriatic coast. The precise date of its construction is not known, but it was probably around 1240, and it was never completed. It's hardly a castle in the real sense of the word. The building does sit on a hilltop, it's true, but it would have been difficult to defend against attack; it has neither a moat nor a drawbridge, for example. The octagonal layout of the limestone building is very unusual, and suggests that the building may have had a far from simple significance. Some of the possible uses that researchers have investigated include hunting lodge, military base, and astronomical observatory.

The Magic Number: Eight

At each of the eight corners of the octagon, there are towers, also octagonal, that are 26 metres (85 feet) high. Two sides of these towers are embedded in corners of the main tower. Small windows have been cut into the walls between the towers and those on the upper floor are decorated with Gothic tracery. The rooms are arranged on two floors around the eight-sided inner courtyard. The system of passages is carefully planned and not all rooms are directly connected with each other: visitors have to cross the courtyard several times in order to reach some of the rooms in the upper storey by way of a spiral stone staircase. The large and imposing entrance gateway on the east side of the complex clearly shows that the emperor wanted there to be no doubt about his claim to power.

Possible prototypes for the unusual Castel del Monte have been discovered in Persia and Anatolia, but the Apulian castle continues to be puzzling. Its eight sides seem to be an image of the imperial crown – one of the four that Frederick II wore. But in ancient times the octagon was also a symbol for the perfection of the cosmos; in Christianity, the number eight stands for the second coming of Christ. Or is the tower possibly a celestial calendar in stone? At certain times of the day or year, certainly, specific shadow groupings cast by the sun and moon can be observed at the castle, and it is well known that Frederick II was interested in the natural sciences, as well as in numerology, magic, philosophy and religion. Whether the idea for Castel del Monte really can be traced back to the learned Emperor's own plans will probably always remain a mystery.

The monumental castle stands proudly on a hill

18 WESTMINSTER ABBEY

In 1245, King Henry III ordered work to begin on the royal abbey church of Westminster; it would take several centuries to complete. The result was the tallest church in England, its nave reaching the imposing height of 32 metres (105 feet) – a church grand enough to be the setting for royal ceremonies to this day.

Westminster Abbey, London, England
From 1245

CHRONOLOGY

With Westminster Abbey, many of the characteristics of French Gothic architecture made their way to the centre of London. That's no surprise, for the church's first master builder was a certain Henry de Reyns (Henry of Reims) – the influence of the architects and stonemasons who were active in Reims in northern France spread to many European countries. This is why, for example, the choir in Westminster is adorned with an ambulatory with radiating chapels, similar to those in French cathedrals. The high windows of Westminster Abbey are supported by an elaborate stone tracery in what is known as the Decorated Style, which made its way across England over the next hundred years. It's named after the lavish decoration that can be found on all parts of the building: the walls and ceiling, the pillars and buttresses, overflow with ornaments.

Gothic Old and New

At the beginning of the 16th century, Henry VI enhanced the east end of the church with a superb chapel, the walls of which are decorated with 95 statues of saints. The most impressive aspect of this chapel is, however, the ceiling, which is covered with fan vaulting. This intricate ceiling structure, with its slender ribs spreading out in a fan shape, was completed in 1509. Fan vaulting of this kind, which is characteristic of the English late medieval period, is described as being in the Perpendicular Style. Two centuries were to pass before the west front of the abbey was given its present appearance. The two flanking towers were not completed until the 18th century, so that here the tracery windows are in a style far more restrained than are those in the much earlier eastern sections of the building.

Princes and the Famous

To this day, the abbey church of Westminster has retained its civic importance. William the Conqueror was crowned in the abbey that stood there before the present one, and since then Westminster has established itself as the site of the coronations and funerals of the English kings and queens. Many other important personalities, including the composer George Frederick Handel and the scientist Isaac Newton, are also buried in the abbey church. One of the most visited of the 3,000 graves in the Abbey is that of the Unknown Soldier, erected in memory of the fallen of the First World War.

The palmette-like ribbed vault spans the central nave

19

THE FORBIDDEN CITY

In building this extraordinary royal palace, the emperors of China were creating a self-contained royal universe remote from the real world. Work began at the beginning of the 15th century, and for the following five centuries it was the only world they knew. Little is known about the builders of the gigantic complex, but the accounts of the highly ritualised life at the Chinese court still fascinate us today.

The Forbidden City, Beijing, China
1406–21

FACT FILE
Area 720,000 sq m / 7,750,000 sq ft
Constructed area 150,000
    sq m / 1,614,585 sq ft
Number of palaces 890
Number of rooms 8,886
Use Imperial palace until 1924; today,
    the Palace Museum

The "crimson" imperial palace gets its name from the red buildings and walls that surround the enormous area. Between 1406 and 1421, around 200,000 workers toiled to build the innumerable palaces and pavilions, gates and gardens, on a site that measures an astonishing 720,000 square metres (7,750,000 square feet). The Chinese believed that the Forbidden City was not only the centre of the Empire, but also the centre of the universe.

A City within a City
The main axis of the palace complex runs from south to north, the Meridian Gate in the south being the main entrance to the palace district. The size of the gate caused the members of a 17th-century Dutch delegation to think that they were standing in front of the entire palace, but in fact they had seen only a fraction of the complex, which has a total of 8,886 rooms. The Meridian Gate leads directly into the government quarters, which could be entered only by ministers, officials and the military. The Golden River, which winds its way through this section of the palace under five marble bridges, represents the five virtues of Confucianism: humanity, honesty, dignity, wisdom and reverence.

A three-tiered terrace leads from a square, which measures 200 x 190 metres (656 x 623 feet), to the Hall of Supreme Harmony. The size of this hall eclipses that of all of the other buildings in the Forbidden City, and no building inside or outside the palace walls was allowed to be taller than its 34-metre (112-feet) Throne Hall. The Emperor held his major audience there three times a year. Dragons, the symbols of his power, can be seen throughout the palace complex.

Strict Protocol
Between 1421 and 1924, 24 emperors and their courts lived behind the high walls, further separated from the common people by a wide moat. The living quarters of the imperial family were located in the northern sector of the complex. And not only they had to be accommodated there: as many as 9,000 ladies-in-waiting, 20,000 eunuchs and 5,000 guards are listed in the court archives as having lived in the palace area. Every step they took was precisely predetermined and the use of the various paths through the complex strictly regulated. Ministers and eunuchs had to approach the Emperor and Empress on their knees, his wives could see the Emperor only by official appointment, and the imperial children were always accompanied by whole processions of servants. They would have been very sorry indeed if one of the imperial children took off and disappeared into the imperial gardens!

The Halls of Harmony on a three-tiered terrace

next pages: The imperial Palace – A view of the Forbidden City from Jingshan hill

61

20

THE DOGE'S PALACE

By the 14th century, more room was needed to house the councillors who governed Venice from the Maggior Consiglio. As their number had risen to 1,800, the former building had become far too small. So, in 1340, the foundation stone of a new seat of government was laid, alongside the Grand Canal.

The Doge's Palace, Venice, Italy
From 1340

CHRONOLOGY

1340   Foundation stone of the new
         Doge's Palace laid
First half 15th C   West wing added
1438–42   Giovanni and Bartolomeo
         Bon build the Porta della Carta
From 1483   East wing built
1559   Palace completed
1577   A fire destroys a major part of
         the palace's pictorial decoration
Second half 16th C   New prison built
1797   End of the Venetian Republic
1811–1904   The Biblioteca Marciana
         housed in the Doge's Palace
Late 19th C   Extensive restoration work
         undertaken
Since 1996   The Doge's Palace is now
         part of a museum, the Musei
         Civici Veneziani

The new meeting room for the city councillors, measuring 54 x 25 metres (177 x 82 feet), was in keeping with the increased demands on space. And, as was the case with all the richly decorated rooms in the Doge's Palace, it was also a place for grand receptions and ceremonies. Paintings by the great Venetian masters, set in elaborate gilded frames, graced the walls and ceilings.

A Naval Power Holds Court
Construction of the palace was to continue into the 17th century. Initially, the west wing was renovated under Doge Francesco Foscari. He had the Porta della Carta built in the north of the palace to provide a connection with St Mark's basilica, and the east wing was added after the fire of 1483, completing the U-form layout of three buildings grouped around an inner courtyard.

The façade of the Doge's Palace is characterized above all by the contrast between the two lower floors, which open outwards as loggias carried by delicate columns and keel arches broken with tracery, and the upper floor, which – with the exception of the lancet windows – is completely covered with red and white marble. Venice's adoption of the Gothic style was determined by its links with the East as well as the West. By the 15th century, the city on the lagoon had become a major marine and trading power, and had particularly close links with the East: influences from the Byzantine Empire had been seen there for a long time. Symbols of Venice's former power on land and sea can be clearly seen in the Doge's Palace: the staircase in the inner courtyard is flanked by two monumental statues of the gods Neptune (sea) and Mars (war).

From the Paper Gateway to the Bridge of Sighs
The impressive size of the Porta della Carta (Paper Gateway), which forms the main entrance to the Doge's Palace, was in keeping with the rich decoration and status of the building. Giovanni and Bartolomeo Bon were commissioned with the construction. High above the entrance stands the Lion of St Mark, in front of which kneels Doge Foscari. A window decorated with tracery rises above this and the gateway ends in a pediment. Sculptures representing the virtues, columns and small knob-like applications decorate the ensemble. The "Paper Gateway" is a surprising name for such a magnificent and important portal. It stems from the fact that petitioners could bring their appeals, written on paper, only as far as this gateway: they were not allowed to enter the palace. The name of the nearby Ponte dei Sospiri (Bridge of Sighs) also hardly seems appropriate for its grand surroundings, until its purpose is understood – it forms the only link to the neighbouring building on the east side of the palace, a prison erected in the 16th century.

The Porta della Carta, main entrance to the Doge's Palace

next pages: Delicate columns and tracery arches characterize the two lower storeys while the upper storey is covered with marble

21 CATHEDRAL DOME IN FLORENCE

In 1418 there was a competition to find a design for the dome of Florence Cathedral. It attracted several artists and architects, for it was a major project, and finally the plans by Filippo Brunelleschi were accepted. In the decades that followed, he performed a superb technical feat in building the dome, though it was an achievement not recognised by those who had commissioned him.

Cathedral Dome, Florence, Italy
1418–36 (Cupola)

Filippo Brunelleschi

1377 Born in Florence
1404 Becomes member of the Florentine Goldsmiths' Guild
1401 Takes part in the competition for the decoration of the door of the Florentine baptistery
1418 Wins competition for the design of the cathedral dome
1419–24 Ospedale degli Innocenti orphanage in Florence
1420 Starts work on the cathedral dome
1420s Old sacristy of San Lorenzo and the Pazzi Chapel, Santa Croce, both in Florence
1436 Commissioned to design a lantern for the cathedral's dome
1446 Dies 16 April in Florence

The building of Florence Cathedral, Santa Maria del Fiore, in the centre of Florence, was making steady progress, but the dome was still to be tackled. And the Florentines wanted something very special: the octagonal drum, the lower section of the dome construction, measures a handsome 45 metres (148 feet) in diameter, so the dome would have to be huge. It was a truly ambitious project: their dome was to be larger that the one that graced the ancient Pantheon in Rome. This spirit of competition was driven not only by a desire to surpass antiquity, but also by the ambition of the important Florentine guilds. The Arte della Lana, the rich wool-workers' guild, was in charge of the construction of the cathedral and they quite clearly wanted to erect a monument that reflected well on them.

Problems Big and Small

With their decision to employ Filippo Brunelleschi, the selection committee had chosen a very experienced master builder. However, they remained sceptical, and gave him control of construction only up to a specific height. Brunelleschi accepted this limitation with fortitude and got down to work. And it was difficult. He was confronted with different problems every day: how, for example, could he get the enormously heavy building materials, sandstone and marble, up to the dizzy heights where they were needed? In response, he invented lifting hoists that were driven by oxen, hoists that had both forward and reverse gears. And so that the workers didn't have to go though the tiring climb down from – and back up to – the dome at midday, he had kitchens and wine store installed under the roof of the church. His main concern, however, was the construction of the dome itself. This, ingeniously, he built in two layers: the inner one carries structural weight, the external provides protection from the weather. This "hollow" design enabled Brunelleschi to reduce the total weight of the vast dome.

Late Recognition

But the members of Arte della Lana were still not convinced. Quite the opposite, in fact. In 1432, when time was drawing near to commission the lantern to crown the dome, they once again organized a competition, and it was only four years later that they were prepared to accept Brunelleschi's model for this final phase of construction. In the meantime, the architect had been harassed by his opponents. He was even thrown into prison for two weeks for working as a builder without belonging to the stonemasons' guild. It was not until after his death in 1446 that the people of Florence recognized his genius and honoured the great architect with a tomb in the heart of the cathedral. His memorial reads: "Here lies the body of a man of great inventiveness, Filippo Brunelleschi of Florence."

View of the cupola and Giotto's campanile

next pages: The cathedral with its massive cupola dominates the townscape of Florence

69

22

THE KREMLIN

Walls, ramparts and towers are the characteristics of a kremlin, the fortified section of a Russian city. However, the example in Moscow, which was constructed from the 14th to the 19th century, is very special: with its palaces and cathedrals it has remained a symbol of Russia's power to this day. It is now a fine museum.

The Kremlin, Moscow, Russia
From 1156

CHRONOLOGY

1156 Start of fortification works

1386 First cathedral built inside the Kremlin

1485–1516 Kremlin extended: enclosed within a brick wall, the Faceted Palace, the Archangel and Dormition cathedrals built

1547 Ivan IV is the first Tsar to be crowned in the Kremlin

17th C Poteshny (Amusement) Palace, Terem Palace and the Cathedral of Twelve Apostles added

1712 Tsar moves his court to St Petersburg

1806 First museum building constructed within the Kremlin

1814 First Kremlin museum opened

1844–51 The Armoury, Russia's treasury, constructed

1918 Lenin orders the return of the government from St Petersburg to the Kremlin

1961 Congress Palace erected

1955 Kremlin (partially) opened for visitors

This former seat of the Russian princes from the 12th century is older than the country it serves today as a political and cultural heart. After 1485, Ivan III speeded up the conversion of the site into a fortified city. He selected Italian architects, who initially devoted themselves to the Kremlin's defence system. Since that time, 2,235 metres (7,330 feet) of a red brick wall, laid out in the form of a triangle, were built around this raised area in the centre of Moscow. Twenty towers, each of them differently decorated, are inserted into the surrounding wall. The main entrance is in the highest of them, the Trinity Tower, on the west side. However, statesmen enter through the Redeemer Tower Gate immediately in front of the government buildings in the north-east of the Kremlin. This tower gets its name from the icon of the Redeemer which originally hung above the gate, and which religious processions filed past. The Arsenal Tower, erected on the massive walls at the northern corner of the Kremlin, is strategically important: the wells in its cellar guaranteed the supply of water in times of siege, and even had a secret passageway that allowed those besieged to leave the Kremlin unseen.

Church Domes and Palaces

The heart of the 28-hectare (70-acre) complex is the rectangular Cathedral Square. In addition to five churches and four palaces, the square boasts an 81-metre (266-feet) tall bell tower from where the largest bell in the world tolled in the 18th century. The bell's 200,000 kilos (nearly 200 tons) of metal, distributed over a diameter of 6.5 metres (21 feet), were shattered following a fall only a few years after its installation. The Kremlin palaces have also been ravaged by time; the largest building had to be reconstructed in the 19th century, and a great number of historical styles were resorted to. The old seat of the tsars, the Terem Palace (erected in 1635/36) can still be admired in all its old glory. Its five storeys are crowned with eleven golden domes that rest on bases covered in green tiles.

The Dormition Cathedral is less playful but considerably more impressive. The tsars passed through the richly decorated south portal to enter their coronation church. Its counterpart is the Church of the Annunciation on the south-west of the square. The many new domes on the former churches of the tsars were an expression of their increasing wealth. After the Russian Revolution, they became museums. However, there is an old Russian saying, "The Kremlin is above the city, but only God is above the Kremlin" – and now religious services are again held in the cathedrals.

The Dormition Cathedral in the Kremlin

The Kremlin houses palaces
and cathedrals

23

ST PETER'S BASILICA

The list of builders who worked on St Peter's in Rome reads like a "who's who" of 16th-century architects. For over a century, this important pilgrimage church, the largest sacred building in Christendom, was designed and redesigned, its many plans redrawn and then discarded ... until, finally, the new St Peter's came into being – a building that embraces the Renaissance, Mannerism and finally the Baroque.

St Peter's Basilica,
Vatican City, Rome, Italy
From 1506

CHRONOLOGY

At the end of the 16th century, Rome was immensely powerful in both the political and cultural spheres. One clear indication of this can be found in the radical urban planning that the Renaissance popes pursued. Streets were laid out, palaces, churches and fountains built, and the Vatican became a major part of the city centre. The most prestigious project of all was St Peter's, which was built above the grave of the Apostle St Peter.

Papal Ambitions
The old St Peter's, the predecessor of today's church, looked back on a history of more than a thousand years, and it was in poor condition. In time, it was also too small. The first plans for the construction of a new Vatican church had already been drawn up in the 15th century. However, it was Pope Julius II who declared that the new St Peter's would finally be built. He was a Pope entirely devoted to supporting the arts – and to ensuring that his fame endured in the form of impressive monuments. In April 1506, Julius had the foundation stone of the new building laid. The architect Donato Bramante had provided the plans: a gigantic central-plan construction in the form of a Greek cross (with four arms of equal length) was envisaged. Later, the architect added a nave to create more space for the congregation, so that the building took on the more traditional form of a church. Julius had announced a special papal indulgence to finance the gigantic project, but the papal plans far exceeded penitents' willingness to donate. When Bramante died in 1514, work on most of the sections had barely begun; in fact, only the choir had progressed. Raphael, Sangallo and, later, Peruzzi were the next architects in charge of construction. Raphael planed a longitudinal layout upon a Latin cross. However, progress was again slow. Luther's attack on the trade in indulgences had important consequences for the new St Peter's: financing their project became even more difficult.

A Baroque Conclusion
It was only when Pope Paul III commissioned Michelangelo with the task of completing St Peter's that work quickened and the basilica finally started to take shape. A huge dome finally crowned the church, which in its size and grandeur would symbolize the growing power and confidence of Catholicism after the Reformation.

In the middle of the 17th century, St Peter's Square, in front of the cathedral, was given its present appearance by the architect and sculptor Gian Lorenzo Bernini. Two ovals in succession, both bordered by rows of huge columns, frame the Baroque façade of St Peter's, designed by Carlo Maderno, and heighten the overwhelming impact of the building.

St Peter's Basilica is crowned by the cupola designed by Michelangelo

The Baroque façade of St Peter's Basilica with the famous central loggia

24

CHÂTEAU OF CHAMBORD

The French king Francis I had recently suffered a political defeat. In 1519, not he but the Hapsburg Charles V had been elected Emperor of the Holy Roman Empire. This event at least settled, for the moment, the struggle for European supremacy.

Château of Chambord, France
From 1519

FACT FILE

Location 320 k/200 miles SW of Paris
Builder Francis I (1494–1547)
Area of the park 5,440 hectares/
   21 sq miles
Number of rooms More than 400
Number of staircases 84
Owner The state, since 1932
1981 UNESCO World Heritage Site
Visitors per year Approx. 800,000

However, this didn't mean that Francis could sit back – there was a need to extend and consolidate his power in France. So at the end of 1519, construction began on a grand royal château in the Loire Valley, where the court and nobility had settled. Francis had a wall built around a 5,500-hectare (13,560-acre) park and woodland, and in the centre of this royal hunting domain he built the Château of Chambord.

"A Utopia in Stone"

This was Prince Metternich's much later description of Chambord. Francis I was particularly fond of contemporary Italian art and architecture and brought many artists from Italy to his court. So it's not surprising that Italian as well as French elements can also be seen in the construction of this "hunting lodge", a description that hardly reflects the château's size and magnificence.

Chambord rises above a base measuring 156 x 117 metres (512 x 304 feet), with the prominent central section being on the north-west side. Similar to the donjons of mediaeval castles, this section stressed the fortress-like character of the château. The central tower is surrounded by three-storeyed side wings; the additional wings were built only to the ground floor level. Four massive round towers are meant to create the impression that the château is well defended. The wide garden at the front of the château, as so often in French grand houses, is set out in strict geometrical order. The extraordinary double spiral staircase, which was completed in 1530, was inspired by Mannerism, a style noted for its use of the irrational or extravagant.

The plans for Chambord probably originated with the Italian Domenico da Cortona, though Jacques and Denis Sourdeau were among the French architects involved in the construction. One other name is connected with the largest of all the Loire châteaux – that of the inventor and artist Leonardo da Vinci: he spent the last years of his life as a guest of Francis I at Amboise, not far away, and it has been suggested that he may have had a hand in the design of Chambord.

Gothic Echoes

Emperor Charles V was enthusiastic when he visited Chambord in 1539; he felt the château to be "the epitome of what human art is capable of achieving". However, at the time, construction had not been completed. In fact, the largest Loire château was never completed, though even in this "unfinished" state it has 440 rooms. The layout was in keeping with contemporary ideas of comfort: the rooms were not arranged in suites but divided into independent, three-room apartments. It is more likely that the Emperor was fascinated above all by the remarkable skyline rather than the interior. There are 365 chimneys, around 800 small turrets, bell towers and oriels rising up from the roofs of Chambord. Reminiscent of the small pointed towers of Gothic cathedrals, these towers and chimneys create a strong impression of a city in miniature.

Staircase, with its double spiral course, in the centre of the main building

King Francis I's hunting lodge – "utopia turned to stone"

25

MACHU PICCHU

The expedition led by the American adventurer Hiram Bingham (probably the original Indiana Jones) had actually set off to the Peruvian Andes in the hope of finding the mysterious Inca city of Vilcamba. What they discovered in summer 1911 proved to be no less sensational.

Machu Picchu, Peru
Start of construction 15th C

CHRONOLOGY

15th C Probable beginning of the
  Machu Picchu complex
ca. 1520 The Inca kingdom reaches it
  greatest expanse
1533 Pizzarro takes the city of Cuzco
1782 Official record of the sale
  of Machu Picchu and the
  surrounding land
1895 A route from Cuzco to Machu
  Picchu established
1911 Academic and explorer Hiram
  Bingham discovers the ruins of
  Machu Picchu
1912/13 Bingham starts excavations
1983 UNESCO World Heritage Site

Three days' march from the old Inca capital city of Cuzco, the group came across ruins overgrown with dense jungle. Could it be Vilcamba? Bingham was convinced it was, and in the following years he had the settlement on the rocky plateau fully excavated. What he'd found became world famous when the National Geographic magazine devoted its entire April 1913 edition to it. The final realisation that it was not Vilcamba did not dampen enthusiasm. What Bingham had really found was even more remarkable: the lost Inca city of Machu Picchu.

Hidden in the Mountains

The Inca probably founded this settlement, which is perched on a mountainside a good 2,300 metres (7,550 feet) above sea level, around the middle of the 15th century. Its purpose and history are shrouded in mystery and very few specific dates are known. According to one theory, Machu Picchu was the residence of the Inca ruler Pachacútec, who settled there with his court and introduced the cult of the sun god Inti. Another theory argues that astronomic calculations were carried out at Machu Picchu. No single explanation is universally accepted.

It seems likely that the complex was probably still under construction a hundred years later when the Spanish conquered the country. Unlike other Inca settlements, however, Machu Picchu remained hidden in the mountains and the city was never looted. However, for some reason the indigenous population abandoned Machu Picchu, taking all their possessions with them.

Terraces and Panoramic Views

More than 200 houses, set in neat rows, have been preserved in Machu Picchu. They were originally connected to each other by a series of narrow streets, pathways and flights of steps. The surrounding land was terraced for agriculture. However, the silos for storing foodstuffs, typical of Inca cities, are missing. Nevertheless, there can be no doubt that people had settled there, for the Machu Picchu complex was clearly divided into a residential area and a temple area. In fact, it's been estimated that approximately 1,000 people could have lived in the city. Some found their final resting place there: since the first expedition, 50 burial sites have been found. The Inca built their living quarters, temples and workshops out of large stones so precisely hewn that they were able to do without mortar. The transport of the huge stones from a nearby quarry was, in itself, another astonishing achievement.

Located high in the Peruvian Andes: Machu Picchu

VILLA LA ROTONDA

In the 16th century, there was scarcely a well-to-do Venetian who didn't want a villa on the mainland. This region, known as the Veneto, was not just a place to relax away from the hubbub of crowded Venice: the fertile land of the Veneto provided Venice with most of its food, and so the fine houses there were often linked with farms.

Villa La Rotonda, Vicenza, Italy
From 1566

Andrea Palladio

1508	Born in Padua, as Andrea di Piero della Gondola
1521	Serves apprenticeship with the stonemason Pietro Cavazza
1524	Settles in Vicenza
1540	Granted the right to call himself an architect
1537	Villa Godi near Vicenza
1542	Palazzo Thiene, Vicenza
1549	Becomes main architect on the renovation of the Palazzo della Ragione, Vicenza
1554	Publishes the guide to the architecture of Rome: *Antichità di Roma*
1565	San Giorgio Maggiore, Venice
ca. 1566	Villa la Rotonda
1570	Published *Four Books on Architecture*
1575	Il Redentore, Venice
1580	Dies 14 August

It was therefore necessary to take the demands of agriculture into consideration when planning villas. Even Andrea Palladio, the most famous villa architect in the Veneto region, included them in his designs. He was inspired above all by the villas of ancient times as recorded by the Roman builder Vitruvius in his treatise on architecture. On his travels to Rome and southern France, Palladio also made a close study of the Roman buildings that had been preserved, and the results can be seen not only in his own designs, but also in his influential writings. In Italy, more than 60 buildings, churches and city palaces, in addition to villas, were based on his plans. But his influence was also felt in other parts of Europe and, as we can see when looking at Jefferson's Monticello (see pages 104–105), in the United States.

The Perfect Form

One of his most famous buildings – and certainly the most copied – is the Villa la Rotonda. Originally called the Villa Almerico-Capra, it was built after 1566 outside the city gates of Vicenza. The name by which it is now known comes from the circular domed hall located exactly in the centre of the villa. The idea of creating a private house as a central-plan building was daring at the time, for this form was generally restricted to sacred buildings. The Rotonda has three floors: the utility rooms were located on the ground floor. The piano nobile, which could be reached by an elegant flight of stairs, was used for entertaining; and the living quarters were located on the mezzanine above. By 1569 the building was almost complete, and its owner, Paolo Almerico, could gaze across the fertile landscape of the region from the luxury of his elegant villa.

From Temple to Villa

Palladio also chose an unusual solution for his decoration of the entrance to the Rotonda by designing it as a temple front: six Ionian columns support a pediment. Palladio describes this design feature in the second of his *Four Books on Architecture*: "In all the villas, and some of the city houses, I have attached the pediment (the temple front) to the façade of the house … in order that these pediments indicate the entrance to the house, and serve also the magnitude and glory of the work in such a way that the front section of the house is elevated above the remaining sections." However, in the Villa la Rotonda, the architect was not satisfied with one temple front: he placed such porticoes on all four sides of the building! By doing without a single main perspective, Palladio stressed the symmetry of the construction: his aim was a classically perfect design in harmony with its setting.

Perfect proportions: The Villa la Rotonda near Vicenza

TAJ MAHAL

Shah Jahan was inconsolable when his beloved wife Mumtaz Mahal died giving birth to her fourteenth child in 1630. After a two-year mourning period, he threw himself into the construction of a building of previously unknown size and grandeur, bringing together the finest builders and craftsmen in north India to construct and decorate it.

Taj Mahal, Agra, India
1632–52

If you want to see the Taj Mahal from your armchair, you can find a comprehensive guide at http://www.taj-mahal.net/newtaj/ There you can enjoy a panoramic overview, from the gatekeeper's lodge to the Garden of Paradise, and from the grave of Mumtaz Mahal to the view from the roof.

Between 1632 and 1652, around 20,000 people were employed in creating the most famous mausoleum in the world. It stands at the northern edge of a garden in Agra, the capital of the Mogul Empire. Shah Jahan chose dazzling white marble as the building material for his wife's tomb. The entrance, however, is in red sandstone, and so stands in marked contrast to the resplendent white façade. The plan is essentially a square with bevelled edges. The building is crowned with an onion dome, flanked by additional cupolas, turrets and slender minarets. The building is also a masterpiece of technology: the dome itself is 65 metres (213 feet) high and 28 metres (92 feet) wide, rising above a cylindrical lower construction, the drum. This dome cannot be seen in the interior; the burial hall is covered by a hemispherical dome. The construction of the central dome was not the only difficulty the builders had to solve; they also had to adapt the interior to cope with the expected flow of pilgrims. Visitors wanted to walk all around the central burial hall, which connects the four side halls.

Place of Pilgrimage

The shah also had plans for his own final resting place: he intended to build a similar palace, this time of black marble, opposite the Taj Mahal. However, his son, who overthrew him in 1658, to prevent the state's bankruptcy, thwarted these plans: he buried Shah Jahan alongside his beloved wife. Even though there is only one mausoleum, the flood of visitors has not ceased to this very day, and millions have admired the building at first hand. Well, that's how it was until 1996. In that year, the heavy basses of a rock concert shook the Taj Mahal so violently that it was weakened. Since then, the building has not been thrown open to large-scale events and, as a precaution, the 350th anniversary celebrations in 2002 were held two kilometres away. Even the pilgrims who want to see the Taj Mahal by moonlight are subjected to strict rules: on five nights each month, no more than 400 of them are allowed to admire India's most famous building from a viewpoint near the palace. If one believes the words of the 19th-century British artist and poet Edward Lear, it is still worthwhile: "In future, the population of our world will be divided into two classes – those who have seen the Taj Mahal, and those who have not."

The Taj Mahal – the mausoleum was intended to be a "memorial to everlasting love"

POTALA PALACE

Located just north of the Himalayas, Lhasa, the former capital of Tibet, stands 3,700 metres (9,800 feet) above sea level. Rising majestically in the centre of the city is the huge Potala Palace complex, one of the few Tibetan cultural monuments to have survived the Chinese Cultural Revolution.

Potala Palace, Lhasa, Tibet
Beginning of construction 17th C

The Potala Palace was added to the UNESCO World Heritage List in 1994. Today, the building is a museum but still belongs to the most important pilgrimage destinations for Tibetan Buddhists.

This palace-monastery completely dominates Lhasa (which means "place of the gods"). It sits on a narrow ridge of the Red Mountain, its southern face built into the rocks that sweep down to the Lhasa River. Due to its location and size, the place complex looks rather like a fortress – it was certainly necessary to have buildings strong enough to combat the cold winds on the roof of the world.

The Spiritual Heart of Tibet

The Potala was the seat of the Tibetan government and official residence of the Dalai Lama, the spiritual and secular leader of Buddhist Tibet, until 1959. The Sanskrit word "Potala" means the seat of the Bodhisattva Avalokiteshvara, and the Dalai Lamas regarded themselves as the mortal embodiment of this being, who was striving for spiritual enlightenment. Today, this palace-monastery complex in Lhasa is a world-famous museum. But along with its most famous temple, the Jokhang Temple, it is still one of the most important places of pilgrimage for Tibetan Buddhists.

The Heart of the Complex

The various palaces and temples in the Potala Palace, which are exemplary for the architecture of this region, cover an area of 300 x 250 metres (984 x 820 feet). The major section of the Potala was constructed during the reign of the fifth Dalai Lama in the second half of the 17th century. The White Palace in the north of the complex, which was built in the short period between 1645 and 1648, forms its heart. The seven-storey building housed the administration and was the Dalai Lama's residence. The largest room of the whitewashed palace, the Great Eastern Assembly Hall, or Tsomchen Shar, on the fourth floor, was used for the New Year's celebrations and the enthronement of the Dalai Lama. It has a surface area of more than 700 square metres (7,535 square feet).

Splendour on the Roof of the World

A dazzling red palace with golden roofs and turrets adjoins on the west, with its numerous temples, chapels and meditation halls. The Dalai Lama's private quarters were also located on the highest of the Red Palace's four storeys. Magnificently decorated *stupas* (Buddhist tombs), where the relics of the deceased Dalai Lamas were preserved, can also be found in the Red Palace. The most magnificent tomb is that of the first builder of the Potala, the fifth Dalai Lama, in the western temple. His tomb is decorated with around 3,700 kilos (8,160 pounds) of gold, as well as precious stones, and rises to a height of more than 14 metres (50 feet) – almost to the palace's roof terrace. Stretched out below is the broad valley of Lhasa.

The Potala Palace on the Red Mountain

VERSAILLES

When Louis XIV, the Sun King, ascended the throne, France had become a new major European power. Its absolutist royal household needed an appropriate home, and so 30,000 workers and all the major artists in the France worked for decades to create it.

Versailles, France
From 1668

Louis Le Vau
1612 Born in Paris, the son of a builder
1642–44 Hôtel Lambert, Paris
1657 Chateau of Vaux-le-Vicomte
1661/62 Reconstruction of the Galérie d'Apollon in the Louvre
1668 Extensions to the palace of Versailles
1670 Dies in Paris

Jules Hardouin-Mansart
1646 Born in Paris
1675 Royal architect
After 1678 Extension of Palace of Versailles, including the Gallery of Mirrors, the Orangerie and Grand Trianon
1680–91 Les Invalides, Paris
Following 1698 Place Vendôme, Paris
1699 Chief court architect
1708 Dies in Marly

André Le Nôtre
1613 Born in Paris; studies painting, architecture and landscape gardening
1656–61 Park of the Chateau of Vaux-le-Vicomte
1661–90 Versailles Park
1700 Dies in Paris

Louis' father had already had a relatively modest hunting lodge constructed in the forest area to the west of Paris. The 'Roi Soleil', by contrast, thought on a completely different scale. In 1668 he commissioned the architect Louis Le Vau to transform the hunting lodge in Versailles into an impressive palace complex. The façade of the new palace was to stretch over 600 metres (1,970 feet). Ten years later, the architect Jules Hardouin-Mansart took over the supervision of the building work. He had the Gallery of Mirrors, which is 71 metres (233 feet) long, built on the first floor on the garden side; this ornate gallery, completely lined with mirrors, was to be used for court balls and receptions. He also built the south and north wings that surround the main court, which is known as the "court of honour". Fifty years – and an astronomical 500 million gold francs – later, construction was finally completed with the court chapel. For the time being, at least. Louis' successor would add an opera house-cum-ballroom that could accommodate 700, as well as two pleasure palaces – the Grand and Petit Trianon – in the northern sector of the spacious grounds.

"L'état c'est moi"

Three main avenues lead to the palace, which forms the central point of a gigantic star-shaped layout. The central point of the castle – and, therefore, of the absolutist cosmos – was the royal bedroom and reception room. It was no coincidence that Louis' motto was "L'état c'est moi" (I am the state). In 1682, the king moved to Versailles with his entire court. Approximately 3,000 people lived in the palace, all observing the strict etiquette of the court, and all organized according to their place in the hierarchy. The royal couple lived on the first floor of the central section, the princes and upper aristocracy in the side wings, facing the park; the less privileged courtiers had to make do with less attractive views.

Art and Nature

At the time construction began, the elevation on which the castle was built was surrounded by swampland. Louis had this land drained, but the cost was high: thousands of workers suffered from yellow fever. Over the next decades, a garden landscape, worked out to the last detail, was created on an area of over 800 hectares (3 square miles) under the supervision of André le Nôtre. Small forests were planted, and two canals dug in order to keep the fountains and waterworks supplied. The area was crossed by symmetrical paths flanked by statues and marble urns. The parterre was formed by rigidly geometrical flowerbeds. Straight rows of clipped trees and sculpturally manicured hedges set the scene – nature transformed by art. Both palace and landscape were now fitting settings for elegant receptions and elaborate royal festivities.

The Hall of Mirrors

The garden façade of the palace

30

ZWINGER PALACE

The Zwinger Palace was originally laid out as a garden on the western border of Dresden, but it soon became the historic centre of the city. Fountains in front of curved façades, staircases adorned with sculptures and balustrades – this "total work of art," created in the exuberant spirit of the Baroque, still impresses.

Zwinger Palace, Dresden, Germany
1709–28

Matthäus Daniel Pöppelmann

1662 Born 3 May in Herford, Westphalia
1686 Settles in Dresden
1705 Appointed state builder to August II the Strong
1705–1915 Taschenberg Palace, Dresden
1711/22 Zwinger, Dresden
1736 Dies 17 January in Dresden

Balthasar Perlmoser

1651 Born 13 August in Kammer in Chiemgau, Bavaria
From 1677 In the service of the Medici in Florence
From 1699 Works as court sculptor in Dresden
From 1712 Sculptural work for the Zwinger in Dresden
1732 Dies 20 February in Dresden

The term "Zwinger" refers to the area or enclosure between two defence walls or ramparts. When Matthäus Daniel Pöppelmann began construction in 1709, the idea was not to build a defence fortification for the city, however, but to provide a setting for magnificent courtly festivities.

Wedding Festivities

Speed was of the essence, as the Zwinger was intended to provide the appropriate setting for a very special wedding in 1719. Prince Frederick August, later king, was to marry the Emperor's daughter, Maria Josepha – an event which required a suitably grand venue. However, the Zwinger was not completely finished at the time of the festivities and the side of the building on Theaterplatz, where the picture gallery is located today, was hidden behind a monumental viewing platform. Contemporaries were nevertheless impressed: "Dreaming of paradise would be no less pleasant", was one observation.

Pavilions and galleries are located around the almost square inner courtyard, in which there are four fountains and where two broad pathways intersect. One leads to the Rampart Pavilion in the north and the Glockenspiel Pavilion in the south. The main entrance is the Crown Gate, a triumphal arch surmounted (appropriately) by a crown-shaped dome.

From Place to Museum

Not all later generations were fond of the late Baroque opulence of the Zwinger. In 1803, the German architect Karl Friedrich Schinkel, who was much more enamoured of the buildings of antiquity, described the Zwinger as "a broad building of ashlars" which was "full of mussels and floral glory in the worst possible style". And indeed Frederick August's taste for elaborate decoration is found everywhere. The main building is covered with stone urns, putti, masks and garlands, and the Nymphs' Bath in the north-eastern section of the complex is particularly rich in sculptural adornment. The nymphs, who give this section its name, stand in the niches of this grotto between cascades, fountains and pools of water. Frederick August commissioned his court sculpture Balthasar Permoser to carve the statues. He himself took care that his collection of art treasures was suitably displayed in the new rooms. The princely collections were a treasure trove of antiques, minerals, scientific instruments and other objects, and can still be admired in the Zwinger today. There's also the armoury, the porcelain collection, and the old-master paintings, for all of which Gottfried Semper erected an extension on the side facing the River Elbe between 1847 and 1855.

A total work of art from the late Baroque period: The Zwinger in Dresden

31

UPPER BELVEDERE

Prince Eugene had worked hard to earn his right to withdraw to his "beautiful view" ("belvedere" in Italian). The field marshal had been successful in the Turkish Wars and had taken the most important Hungarian fortress in Budapest. It was time to build a monument to himself.

Upper Belvedere, Vienna, Austria
1721–23

Johann Lukas von Hildebrandt

1668	Born 14 November in Genoa, Italy
1695/96	Serves as field engineer in Upper Italy
1696	Settles in Vienna
1697	Garden palace Mansfeld-Fondi (today, Palais Schwarzenberg)
1700–13	Works as court engineer in Vienna
1714–16	Lower Belvedere
1723	Becomes court architect
1721–22	Upper Belvedere
1730s	Residence in Würzburg
1745	Dies 16 November in Vienna

Vienna had successfully warded off the Turkish threat and by 1683 the Ottoman Empire was finally defeated. The city came to life: the population increased, ambitious building projects were undertaken, and "Vienna Gloriosa" blossomed. The opulent Baroque style was well suited to the optimism and grandeur of the period. The aristocracy was now finally able to devote itself to fine houses, and the Glacis – an undeveloped area intended to protect the city – was made available as building land. The Austrian general Prince Eugene of Savoy had no intention of missing this opportunity, particularly as his military successes had made him one of the most influential men in the country.

Palace after Palace

Prince Eugene decided to have a garden palace erected on land he owned near the city wall. Between 1714 and 1716, his personal architect, Johann Lukas von Hildebrandt, created the Lower Belvedere – a Baroque summer residence with rooms for daily living and for entertaining, an orangery, and magnificent stables.

However, Eugene's passion for building was not satisfied. Five years later, after the prince had recently retired from military service, Hildebrandt tackled the Upper Belvedere, which lay on a higher section of the terraced garden area. The prince had originally planned a small building that would provide a focal point for his estate. The final result, however, went far beyond the scope of a small garden palace. The building itself consists of several huge pavilions, each of which is of a different height. The corner buildings, with their domed roofs, are particularly prominent. The central section of the palace, with its grand pediment and rich sculptural ornamentation, is particularly impressive – especially when reflected in the artificial lake just in front of the palace.

Palace and Museum

A magnificent staircase leads from the entrance hall on the ground floor to the centre of the building, the Marble Hall, which is richly decorated with stucco and frescoes. No time was wasted in completing the Upper Belvedere, and the lavish interior décor was in place by 1723. The Prince's library and art collection were located on the ground floor of the building. Both palaces are now part of a museum, the Österreichische Galerie, with its collections ranging from the Middle Ages to contemporary art. The symmetrical park that links the two places is no less ornate. The fountains, paths and flowerbeds are inhabited by numerous gods hewn in stone. In addition to the leader of the muses, Apollo, the eternal victor Hercules is prominently represented – entirely fitting in a palace built for a military leader.

The sala terrena on the ground floor

The representative garden façade of the palace with the complex of ponds in front of it

32

THE LOUVRE

Countless builders were occupied for centuries on this building complex in the heart of Paris. The Louvre was transformed from a castle into a palace, and then from a royal residence into one of the largest museums in the world.

The Louvre, Paris, France
Beginning of construction 12th century

FACT FILE

Main building period 1546 to mid 18th C
Use Museum, since 1793
Exhibition space 60,000 sq m / 645,830 sq ft
Number of artworks Approx. 35,000
Departments Oriental Antiquities; Egyptian Antiquities; Greek, Etruscan and Roman Antiquities; Islamic Art; Sculptures; Objets d'art; Paintings; Prints and Drawings
Visitors Approx. 10 million annually

At the end of the 12th century, King Philippe II had Paris – at the time, the largest city in Europe – fortified: a rectangular castle with a solitary round tower was erected on the right bank of the Seine. Philippe's successors had other ideas, however, and the castle was merely to be the modest foundation for what today is the Louvre.

From Castle to Palace

Francis I was a great admirer of Italian Renaissance architecture and in 1546 commissioned the court architect Pierre Lescot to carry out large-scale renovations based on Italian models. The result was more like a new building than a renovation, for the King had the entire west section of the castle demolished and rebuilt. The intention was to convert the medieval castle into a modern palace. A four-sided court, flanked by two-storey buildings, was planned, but Lescot was able to complete only the west and southern sections, which were richly decorated with sculptures by the leading sculptor Jean Goujon. The windows of the two floors are framed with pediments, and the magnificent doorways are reminiscent of ancient triumphal arches.

In the 17th century, work commenced on the east wing. The celebrated sculptor and architect Gian Lorenzo Bernini, a leading representative of Italian Baroque, submitted plans, but the commission was finally granted to the French architect Claude Perrault, who designed a magnificent colonnade. However, Louis XVI was now becoming more and more interested in another project, the extension of the palace at Versailles (see pages 92–95). The Louvre had outlived its usefulness as a royal residence. Junk dealers settled in the courtyard, the royal academies took over many of the rooms that had already been completed, and artists used the remaining rooms as studios. It was not until the middle of the 18th century that the courtside façade of the Cour Carré was completed. After this, a lack of funds prevented further building. It had taken on its present appearance by the middle of the 18th century.

From Palace to Museum

The fate of the Louvre was sealed in 1793, the year of the French Revolution. The doors of the former royal palace were thrown open as the first public art museum. Five years later, the Musée d'Architecture was installed in its elegant rooms. However, artists still determined life in the Louvre; it was difficult to rid itself of its role as a gigantic studio. In order to create space for the artworks that Napoleon had seized as he invaded one European country after another, the architects Charles Percier and Pierre-François-Léonard Fontaine began the construction of the north wing.

In 1981, under President Mitterand, the decision was taken to use all of the rooms as a museum. The Louvre was once again turned into an enormous building site. This time, the American-Chinese architect Ieoh Ming Pei was in charge, and since 1989 his glass pyramid in the centre of the Cour Napoléon has formed the striking entrance to the Louvre.

The glass pyramid in front of the Louvre, created by the architect Ieoh Ming Pei

33

MONTICELLO

Thomas Jefferson gave his property just outside the small town of Charlottesville the mellifluous name of Monticello. Begun around 1770, this country house, following the formal language of Italian models, was built on the "small mountain" in the midst of an old tobacco plantation.

Monticello, Charlottesville, USA
ca. 1770

Thomas Jefferson

1743 Born 13 April in Albemarle County, Virginia
1760s Studies law
From 1767 Works as an attorney
1772 Marries Martha Wayles Skelton
1774 Becomes Representative for Virginia in Congress. Works on the colonies' Declaration of Independence
1779–81 Governor of Virginia
1785–89 Serves as diplomat in France; after his return to the USA, becomes Foreign Minister
1785–92 Virginia State Capitol built to his design
1796 Becomes Vice President
1801–09 Serves as third President of the USA
1826 Dies 4 July in Monticello, Virginia

The governor of Virginia, foreign minister and later the third president of the United States, Jefferson was a man of many talents. He was interested in the natural sciences and philosophy, and was an amateur archaeologist. And despite his work as a lawyer and politician, he still found time to devote himself to building. In addition to public buildings, including the University of Virginia, Jefferson took on the planning of his own country seat. History played a key role in his designs: the United States was still a young Republic, and its culture, politics and architecture drew upon principles of ancient Republican Rome. The epitome of ancient Roman architecture was the Pantheon, a temple consecrated to all the Gods.

Perfect Harmony

The main entrance seems better suited to a Roman temple than a country house: sturdy columns support a profiled cornice on which rests a pediment. Two side wings on the left and right recede from the prominent portico. The white columns and window frames contrast effectively with the red of the bricks. The central dome, rising behind the portico, is also white. Harmony was the guiding principle, and the entire complex is exactly symmetrical. Columned vestibules on both the front and back of the house lead into the interior, and everywhere horizontal and vertical elements complement each other in perfect harmony.

Renaissance Inspiration

Thomas Jefferson was not the first person to value ancient buildings as a source of inspiration. Renaissance architects in particular had studied them closely. One of these was the Italian architect Andrea Palladio, who in the 16th century built numerous country villas in the Veneto region close to Venice. It was his designs in particular that served as models in the 18th century. His Villa Rotonda, a central-plan building near Vicenza, is one of his most ingenious and influential designs (see pages 86–87). Jefferson was greatly attracted to Palladio's restrained classicism when designing Monticello. He withdrew to this country seat when he retired from politics, though it was not to enjoy a quiet life. He had many cultural and scientific interests, as shown by his library, which contained more than 6,000 volumes on all manner of subjects. These would later form the basis for the collection of the Library of Congress in Washington, D.C.

The President's country house: Monticello near Charlottesville

34

ROYAL CRESCENT

Bath, a small town in the west of England, developed into a fashionable spa in the 18th century. The city planners faced the task of trying to create an attractive and well-organised urban environment that met all the needs of their wealthy guests.

Royal Crescent, Bath, England
1767–74

John Wood the Younger
1728   Born 25 February in Bath
1754–64 Continues with The Circus,
       begun by his father
1767–74 Builds Royal Crescent
1769–71 Builds Assembly Halls in Bath
       (today the Costume Museum)
1781   Dies 18 June in Bath

The house at number 1 Royal Crescent is now a museum and gives a vivid impression of the interior decoration of the houses on the crescent in the 18th century.

The writer Johanna Schopenhauer, the mother of the celebrated German philosopher Arthur Schopenhauer, stayed in Bath during her trip to England in 1787, and reported that "the entire city is an enormous hôtel garni". Hotels, theatres, ballrooms and coffee houses were erected as social meeting places, promenades created for the essential "stroll through the town", and the roads carrying visitor and goods around the town were greatly improved. Above all, more housing was needed: the population of what had become the most important British spa increased tenfold during the 18th century.

Father and Son

John Wood the Younger, following in his father's footsteps as an architect, played an important role in creating the city's new appearance. John Wood the Elder had planned Queen Square, followed around the middle of the century by The Circus, with its circular plan. In 1767, his son started work on the row of houses to be called the Royal Crescent, located not far from The Circus. The name comes from the shape of the row, which resembles that of a crescent moon. This semi-circular row of large urban villas lies on a slope in the large Royal Victoria Park. The open side of the crescent faces a broad lawn and provides a fine view of the city. Here the architect had turned his back on the contemporary ideals of urban construction, which favoured closed forms.

Classical Inspiration

The fronts of the 30 houses of the Royal Crescent (which in effect create a singe façade) are decorated in exactly the same way. The ground floor, above the basement, which was originally planned for the staff, is not subdivided. The upper storeys, by contrast, have tall Ionian columns between the windows. These half-columns stretch over two storeys, in a style known as the "giant order". The absence of any further accentuation of individual building components is typical of the Georgian era, when the building boom in Bath took place. The symmetrical structure of the façade and floor plan is typical for this restrained style, as is a return to the architecture of classical antiquity, which can be seen above all in the columns and arches. Though there is now a hotel in the centre of the Royal Crescent, most of the houses are still family homes, and still enjoy a fine view of the city.

Royal Crescent – a semi-circular row of houses

35

UNITED STATES CAPITOL

The dazzling white Capitol stands proudly at the eastern end of Washington's National Mall. It was planned as the seat of government of the – then very young – United States, yet its builders looked back to the Europe of ancient times for inspiration.

United States Capitol, Washington, D.C., USA
From 1793

CHRONOLOGY

1793 Foundation stone laid by George Washington

1801 The Supreme Court meets in the Capitol for the first time

1803 Benjamin Henry Latrobe commissioned by President Jefferson to continue construction

1810 The Senate moves into the north wing

1814 British troops burn the Capitol to the ground

1815–17 Latrobe begins the reconstruction

1818 Charles Bulfinch becomes Latrobe's successor

1819 Supreme Court, Senate and House of Representatives meet in the Capitol

1850 Competition for extensions to the Capitol held

1851 Foundation stone laid for the extensions planned by the architect Thomas U. Walter

1865 Walter completes the dome

1935 The Supreme Court receives its own building

In 1776, the 13 foundation states of the United States declared themselves independent of Britain. This led to a great increase in the number of new buildings, particularly those for the new government institutions. The parliament building was to be the chief expression of the social and political ideals of the country. Ancient Greece and Rome provided both the political and architectural inspiration, with the Capitol becoming one of the finest examples of American Neo-Classicism.

In Rome's Footsteps

It was intended that the representatives of the American people should meet on Capitol Hill, named after the most important of the Seven Hills of Rome. The parliament was named the Senate – an additional indication of the influence of ancient Rome. In 1793, George Washington finally laid the cornerstone for the Capitol: the city of Washington was later built around it.

The young architect William Thornton was responsible for the plans. However, the list of architects and builders became longer and longer as various renovations and extensions were undertaken over the following decades. The building soon proved to be too small to accommodate the representatives of all the states. It was originally planned for the 13 founding states, but the number had more than doubled since the beginning of construction. The size of the Capitol was doubled accordingly: two additional parts were created for the Senate and House of Representatives.

The circular central building is approximately 60 metres (200 feet) high, with columned vestibules to the east and west. North and south wings were added later. A flag indicates which house is in session. Thomas Walter crowned the building with the huge dome in 1865. To this day, it has remained the emblem not only of the capital city but also of the American belief in progress: Walter used 4,000 tons of cast iron – a completely new building material at the time – for the two shells forming the dome.

A Quick Tour

The Capitol is not merely a building: it's a city within a city. Every working day, around 20,000 people make their way between the Dome and the six Legislative Buildings, and it's not difficult to get lost in the 850 corridors. The many millions of visitors who come to Capitol Hill every year are drawn there not only by the offices and assembly halls, but also by an impressive art collection. The Capitol is guarded by its own police, who keep a close eye on the large number of demonstrators who want to draw attention to their causes in front of this symbol of America's political life and national identity.

View of the Capitol dome inside

The Capitol is the geographical central point of Washington;
its cupola is still the city's emblem

36

LA SAGRADA FAMÍLIA

One of the world's most famous buildings, the church of La Sagrada Família (Catalan for "Holy Family") is situated in the centre of the Spanish city of Barcelona. The architect Antoní Gaudí y Cornet devoted three decades of his life to the building of the church, and it may not be completed until 2050.

La Sagrada Família, Barcelona, Spain
Beginning of construction 1882

Antoni Gaudí y Cornet
1852 Born in Reus, Catalonia, Spain
1878 Completes architecture studies in Barcelona
1883–85 Villa Quijano (El Capricho) in Comillas, Cantabria; Casa Vicens, Barcelona
1883–1926 La Sagrada Família, Barcelona
1886–90 Palacio Güell, Barcelona
1887–93 Archbishop's Palace in Astorga, León
1889–90 Colegio de las Teresianas, Barcelona
1900–14 Park Güell, Barcelona
1904–06 Casa Batlló, Barcelona
1906–10 Casa Milà (La Pedrera), Barcelona
1926 Dies in Barcelona

The beginning of his career was not very promising: the Catalan Gaudí graduated from university with the lowest grade possible, a mere "pass". However, he soon found an influential client in the entrepreneur Eusebi Güell, and made a name for himself with numerous buildings in Barcelona. In 1883, when Gaudí started working on the Sagrada Família (he was only 33 years old), the crypt was already under construction. The neo-Gothic plans for the church had been drawn up by the architect Francisco de Paula del Villar y Lozano, who had started construction one year before. Gaudí continued with Gothic forms, but not for long. His inspiration was not the architecture of the Middle Ages, but nature: the pillars and supports look like trees, with their branches and stone leaves, and there are flowers, insects and other creatures everywhere. Gaudí decided on round forms and extravagant, knob-like capitals for the planned 12 bell-towers – one for each of the Apostles. Colour symbolism was also given its due: the Door of Hope on the west was planned to glow in hues of green.

A Sermon in Stone

The basic shape of the Sagrada Família is a cross, but the circle is almost more important. According to Gaudí: "The straight line is the line of mankind; the curve is the line of God." His notion of a "sermon in stone" may explain why he devoted so much space to the sung praise of God: there's room for 1,500 singers in the galleries and five organs.

Potentially, at least. When the architect died in a road accident in 1926, most of the information on the Sagrada Família was in the form of plans and a plaster model. Only one of three façades – on the east – was under construction, and the east portal, with its depiction of the Nativity, was not yet completed. Even today, the towers – the highest is planned to soar 170 metres (558 feet) into the sky – still stand side by side with construction cranes. This is not just because of Gaudí's complicated plans, which are full of detail and rich in symbolism. The Sagrada Família was planned as a "penance church", to be built exclusively from voluntary contributions. Particularly during the First World War, the financial resources available for the building work were meagre, and Gaudí himself had to help find people willing to make donations. The church has consumed incredible sums and even now is making only slow progress. Gaudí would probably bear it with fortitude: he understood that "God is not in a hurry".

La Sagrada Família – still unfinished today

37

THE EIFFEL TOWER

In 1889, no one expected that this temporary metal tower would become the symbol of Paris, and indeed France. Quite the contrary: the Eiffel Tower, which had been constructed for the Paris World Exposition, was widely ridiculed. The writer Guy de Maupassant considered the tower a "skinny pyramid of iron ladders" – and that was almost a compliment.

The Eiffel Tower, Paris, France
1887–89

Gustave Eiffel

1832 Born in Dijon
1867 Maison Eiffel
1876 Engineer on the construction of the Bon Marché department store, Paris
1877 Bridge over the Douro
1880–84 Garabit Bridge
1885 Participates in the building of the Statue of Liberty in New York
1889 Eiffel Tower
1923 Dies in Paris

Though almost 300 metres (984 feet) high, this metal construction – for many years the tallest building in the world – was erected in a mere two years. The tower was made of 12,000 individual parts held together by 2.5 million rivets. Eiffel and his colleagues required 5,300 drawings to plan the construction. Their design and their construction techniques guaranteed maximum stability with minimum weight. But not everybody was convinced. One man living on the Champs de Mars nearby went to court out of fear that the tower could collapse on his house. That was not the only concern troubling Eiffel's contemporaries. Critics initially called the building a "tragic lamp-post" and talked about "a disgusting column of riveted metal".

Its Many Uses

The use of iron as a construction material was, in itself, novel. And not hiding this framework behind stone or brick was revolutionary. Four columns rise up from a square base and finally come together to form a peak at a dizzy height. A network of struts fills the area in between the columns to give the structure great strength and stability. The four large arches at the base were added later because the critics thought that the tower looked bare.

Another criticism was that this metal tower, which was originally meant to be a temporary structure, had no real function. Well, at least science found a use for it, when an observatory and laboratory for the collection of meteorological data were added. And above all it became a major tourist attraction. A platform with restaurants and sales booths was located 57 metres (187 feet) above the ground, and there was an additional opportunity for seeing Paris from above at a height of 115 metres (377 feet). Its eight lifts transported 4,200 visitors – those who found the 1,710 stairs too wearisome – every day. And, in 1921, the antenna on the Eiffel Tower transmitted Europe's first public radio broadcast.

Upward Investment

The entrepreneur Eiffel bore the lion's share of the costs of 6.5 million francs himself and so had the right to use the tower for 20 years. The two million paying visitors during the World Exposition soon made it clear that it would be a worthwhile investment for Eiffel, who had already started to make a profit by 1890. And he was proven right with his reasons for his plan: "The tower can be seen as worthy of representing the art of the modern engineer and the century of industry and science, whose foundations were laid during the Revolution of 1789."

The Eiffel Tower, built for the 1889 World Exposition

38

SULLIVAN CENTER

Chicago, the birthplace of the skyscraper, can boast a great many exceptional examples of modern architecture. Among the architects who changed the face of the city in the last quarter of the 19th century, by far the most influential was Louis Henry Sullivan.

Sullivan Center, Chicago, USA
1899–1904

Louis Henry Sullivan

1856   Born in Boston. Studies at the Massachusetts Institute of Technology

1873   Moves to Chicago

1874/75   Studies in Paris

1881   Becomes partner of the architect and engineer Dankmar Adler

1886–89   Auditorium Building, Chicago, in collaboration with Adler

1890/91   Wainwright Building, St Louis

1894–96   Guarantee Building, Buffalo, in collaboration with Adler

1899–1904   Schlesinger & Mayer Store, Chicago (today Carson Pirie Scott Building)

1924   Dies in Chicago

It was Sullivan's conviction that a building should show what went on inside it: its function, whether warehouse, office or home. There was nothing wrong with decoration, insisted Sullivan, as long as it harmonized with the function: structure, function and appearance should be in complete harmony. He had a very clear conception of the skyscraper, which was still in its infancy: "It has to be high, every inch of it has to be high. The strength and force of the height must be integral to it – the magnificence and pride of enthusiasm."

Chicago Shoots Up

Chicago was the ideal city for the Boston-born architect. After the Great Fire of 1871, it was necessary to erect many new buildings in a short time, and they had to be modern and in-expensive. And in order to keep to the existing plan of the city, development had to be upwards: there was little room to spread outwards. Chicago's first steel-framed building – the Home Insurance Building – was erected in the 1880s. As the steel frame carried the main weight of a building, there was no longer any need for thick walls, and so architects now had greater liberty to decorate the façades. This building technique also made it possible to greatly increase the number of windows, a fact important in the development of the department stores, which were then just beginning. In the following years, additional commercial and office buildings made of metal and glass shot up. Between 1899 and 1904, Sullivan created one of the most important buildings of the Chicago School – the Sullivan Center, formerly known as the Schlesinger & Meyer Store and then the Carson Pirie Scott Building, which was built as a department store.

Glass and Steel

The rich ornamentation of the two lower floors of the building contrasts greatly with the simplicity of those above. In these upper floors, both the horizontal and vertical lines are strongly emphasised, creating a cell-like appearance (all the more pronounced because the windows are deeply recessed). These lines in effect reveal rather than conceal the underlying structure of the building, a fact that reflects a new honesty in designs. The bold, almost brutal, linearity of the façades is softened by the main corner, which is round. It is at the bottom of this tower-like feature than the main entrance to the department store is located. Unlike most of the building, this entrance is elaborately decorated with wrought iron, and so is a clear focal point at ground level. The entrance and elaborate display windows are meant to encourage passers-by to gaze into, and then enter, this temple of commerce.

The Sullivan Center – lavish ornamentation of the two lower storeys

BAUHAUS

Bauhaus, Dessau, Germany
1925–26

Walter Gropius

1883 Born 18 May in Berlin

1903–07 Studies at the Technical Universities of Munich and Berlin

1907–10 Works as Peter Behrens' assistant in Berlin

1910 Becomes a freelance designer

1911–13 Redesigns the Fagus Shoe Factory, with Adolf Meyer

1916 Marries Alma Schindler Mahler

1919 Teaches at the University for Fine Arts in Weimar (renamed Bauhaus)

1919–30 Siemensstadt, Berlin

1928 Relinquishes his directorship of the Bauhaus; opens his own office in Berlin

1934 Goes into exile in England

1937 Takes up position at Harvard University

1958–63 Pan American Building, New York

1969 Dies 5 July in Boston

Cubic building elements, clear white surfaces and symmetric rows of windows – Gropius' buildings appear to be severe and entirely functional. His approach dominated the curriculum of the school and caused a worldwide sensation as the "International Style". It was above all through his design for the Bauhaus building that his influence spread. So it's hard to believe that this sought-after architect was a not natural draughtsman: as a student, he wrote to his mother that he was "not capable of drawing a straight line".

Good Design at Affordable Prices

This had no effect on his later designs, however (he always had assistants for drawing up plans!). His designs, which included both industrial and residential projects, were based on the belief that well-designed buildings could be made inexpensively through the use of standardised, prefabricated elements to be assembled, literally, like building blocks – good quality mass production for the masses. His plans included satellite towns and residential high-rise buildings, ideas violently criticized at the time. His guiding principle was that "artistic design is not a luxury but must always be a part of life itself". He brought these ideas into the designing of the Bauhaus building, which is one of the best examples of his architecture. It had to be built when the Bauhaus School moved to Dessau in 1925. It's an elegant, eminently functional building in which all aspects of design and purpose are perfectly united.

A Home for the Bauhaus

This asymmetric building, which still appears thoroughly modern, was his manifesto in concrete, steel and glass. According to the 1919 manifesto of the Bauhaus, the aim was to have artists, designers, architects, sculptors and painters working together at the school in order to develop the "new buildings of the future".

The building has three linked L-shaped wings. The workshop wing, which bears the vertical name "Bauhaus" in large letters, is notable for its glass curtain-wall, a feature that gave it the popular name "the Aquarium". This leads directly to a low building where kitchens, canteen and gymnasium are located; and this in turn leads to the much higher accommodation block, on which there's a roof-garden. Linking these blocks with the large Schools of Arts and Crafts is a two-storey bridge wing that passes over a road. This wing became the School of Architecture. Unlike the workshop, with its glass wall, this connecting wing and the School of Arts and Crafts have long horizontal rows of windows, and are of a light colour. The windows in the accommodation wing have small balconies. Throughout the complex, interior features and fittings were designed down to the last detail. Purpose-built as a school of art and design, the Bauhaus building embodies the groundbreaking ideas of Gropius and his school – a building in which art, craft and modern technology work in harmony. The result was one of the most influential buildings of 20th-century architecture.

The Bauhaus – the name of the art school soon developed into a stylistic expression

The Bauhaus in Dessau, strictly functional

40

CHRYSLER BUILDING

For a short time, this building was the highest in the world. The urban historian Lewis Mumford said: "Heaven help whoever looks up at this building without being far enough away from it and helped by thick fog." Hard words for the 319-metre (1,050-feet) high Chrysler Building in Manhattan, which started to take shape in October 1928.

Chrysler Building, New York City, USA
1928–30

FACT FILE

Location 405 Lexington Avenue, corner of 42nd Street
Architect William van Alen (1882–1954)
Planning of supporting structure Ralph Squire & Sons
Height 319 m / 1,050 ft
Height of steel spire 55 m / 180 ft
Total weight Approx. 112,000 tons
Number of storeys 71
Lifts 34
Use Office space

Wedding Cake

Three thousand workers laboured in double shifts on the prominent building site opposite the Grand Central Station. Top priority was given to safety and there were no serious accidents during the concentrated building work. First, it was necessary to dig 21 metres (70 feet) into the ground to set the foundations, which have to support 112,000 tons spread over 71 floors. The rectangular base takes up the entire site but the building itself tapers upwards. This "wedding cake style" was widespread in New York in the 1920s, thanks to the new building regulations: it was possible to construct new buildings of great height only if the tower, above the thirteenth floor, took up one-quarter of the area of the base. The aim of the first owner, William H. Reynolds, who soon sold the building to Walter P. Chrysler, was for his new building to surpass the height of the Eiffel Tower in Paris (see pages 114–115) – and he was successful. After some 4,000 windows and almost 3,000 doors had been installed, seven scale-like Art Deco arches were attached to each side of the tower at the top of the building. A steel spire 55 metres (180 feet) long rises out of the tower. In 1931, this spire made the Chrysler Building the highest in the world. But not for long: it was soon surpassed by the Empire State Building, also in New York.

Art Deco

"No old stuff for me. No corrupt copies of gates, columns and oriels. I – I am new! Avanti." The Architect William van Allen was in no way traditional: modern ideas were given priority – from the disposal of garbage in record time, to the radiators recessed in the walls. After William H. Reynolds had handed the project over to the automobile tycoon Walter P. Chrysler, the glittering façade became representative of the mood of the Jazz Age: zigzag patterns, triangles and rectangles of light grey tiles and white marble decorate the building. The metal eagle heads, hubcaps, radiator grilles and other parts reminiscent of cars in the recesses of the building make a clear reference to the man who owned the building. Here, modern technology joined hands with Art Deco to form an extravagant design – the decoration of the exterior of the Chrysler Building was just as important as the decoration of its interior. This approach had its keen admirers: Paul Goldberger, the architecture critic of the *New York Times*, found the building "romantic and irrational, and yet not quite so foolish as to be laughable; it stops just short of that and maintains a bit of credibility in its folly – just like New York itself".

The Chrysler Building was the highest edifice in the world until the Empire State Building was constructed.

Lift door with Art Deco ornaments

right: Aerial view of the Chrysler Building

CASA MALAPARTE

In 1938, a long, red-plastered rectangular building started to take shape on the Punta Massullo. This house juts out to the tip of a bare rock overhang below which the rugged cliff falls steeply into the sea. The Italian authorities had made this single exception for Curzio Malaparte – as the Italian writer and journalist Kurt Erwin Suckert had named himself.

A House as a Portrait

He made his decision the moment he saw the spot. And as it was generally assumed that the plot of land he had found could not be built on, it was at least very inexpensive. But Curzio Malaparte was well connected to the Fascist Party – and Mussolini's son-in-law in particular – and so he was able to begin construction a mere three months after his arrival on Capri.

Building permission had been given, but it was also necessary to submit the plans drawn up by the architect, Adalberto Libera. His task was not an easy one, for Malaparte never grew tired of stressing his personal authorship of the building. The house on the rocks, he said, was a portrait of himself – all he had needed was "a little help" from a builder on the island. However, it's a matter of record that it was Libera who settled on the basic rectangular form, and on the spectacular open terrace. A staircase, which becomes wider as it ascends, leads up to it. The curious curved concrete wall on the roof, which is plastered white, forms an effective contrast to the warm red of the rest of the house. Its purpose was to provide shelter from the fierce sun. It's also said that Malaparte like to ride his bicycle on the roof – perhaps he also wanted to prevent the curious from seeing him.

A Beautiful Setting

The Casa Malaparte offers many fine views. The differently sized windows are placed asymmetrically along the walls and allow countless views of the countryside and sea from the interior. The living room, covering more than 100 square metres (1,070 square feet) on the second floor of the low building, occupies most of the area of the house. There are also plenty of guest rooms, and in spite of – or maybe because of – the remote location, many visitors did indeed come to Casa Malaparte. One of them was the film director Jean-Luc Godard, who in 1963 chose the house as the setting for his film *Le Mépris* ("Contempt"), which starred Brigitte Bardot and Michel Piccoli.

Malaparte himself, once condemned as a Fascist, later made headlines once again. In old age, he turned to Communism and left the house on the fisherman's island to the communist Chinese government in gratitude for their hospitality during his stay in China. Malaparte's relatives contested the will and were ultimately successful.

View of the property from the cliff path

42

THE GLASS HOUSE

The architect Philip Johnson's glass house stands on a broad expanse of lawn surrounded by high, isolated trees. The unpretentious building looks less like a dwelling than a glass box, and seems to enhance or frame the landscape rather than to intrude upon it.

The Glass House, New Canaan, USA
1947–49

Philip Cortelyou Johnson

1906 Born 8 July in Cleveland
1927 Graduates in philology at Harvard
1930 Founds the Architecture and Design Department of the Museum of Modern Art, New York
1932 Publishes *The International Style: Architecture Since 1922*, with Henry-Russell Hitchcock
1940 Begins to study architecture (teachers include Walter Gropius and Marcel Breuer)
1946–54 Head of the Architecture Department of the Museum of Modern Art
1947–50 Glass House, New Canaan
1954–58 Seagram Building, New York (concept: Mies van der Rohe)
1967 Begins collaboration with John Burgee
1979 Wins Pritzker Prize
1980–84 AT&T Headquarters, New York
1988 Co-organizes *Deconstructivist Architecture* exhibition
1995 Gate House, New Canaan
2005 Dies 12 September in New Canaan

Philip Johnson had made a name for himself mainly as a theoretician. As head of the architecture department of the New York Museum of Modern Art, he published the catalogue *The International Style: Architecture Since 1922*, together with Henry-Russell Hitchcock, for an exhibition of the same name. They were attempting to find common characteristics of modern European architecture, such as the elimination of any ornamentation. Johnson was to carry this to the extreme with the radical simplicity of his own house.

Walls? Forget them!

But first, and now already in his mid-thirties, he started studying architecture. Walter Gropius, the influential Bauhaus architect, was one of his professors (see pages 118–119). This could not remain without consequences for the budding architect; and when Johnson began constructing his own house in Connecticut in 1947 he set new standards in minimalism. One looks for walls in vain: nature itself seems to set the boundaries of the building – the supporting steel frame is hardly visible, and all the surfaces between the frames are of uninterrupted glass. A brick cylinder is the only opaque element: this houses the technical installations and the bathroom. Its red form rises a little above the flat roof and is the only – and very discreet – spot of colour in the one-space house, which is completely assimilated into its surroundings.

Mies van der Johnson

Steel and glass were the two materials that made it possible for architects to dematerialise their buildings to the extent that there is hardly any perception of an enclosed space. A few years previously, the architect Mies van der Rohe had investigated the concept of "flowing spaces", rooms without any walls. Johnson modelled his building on van der Rohe's glass Farnsworth House, in Illinois. He had recently devoted an exhibition in MoMA to the German-born architect and, in the 1950s, they were jointly to build the New York Seagram Building, a landmark in modern architecture. Some found this degree of co-operation a little curious, and for a while Philip Johnson was nicknamed "Mies van der Johnson". His glass house design, however, did have its admirers, and this generously laid-out house, flooded with light, was admired by many architects, designers and even clients.

The Glass House – nature forms the borders of the building

43 NOTRE DAME DU HAUT

The local press condemned Le Corbusier's plans for this chapel as "religious rubbish", and as looking like a "slipper". This was no surprise: nowhere was there a sign of a right angle, a straight side or symmetrical façade. Nevertheless, the chapel of Notre Dame du Haut has long since changed from being a "pile of concrete" into an architectural icon.

Notre Dame du Haut, Ronchamp, France
1950–54

Le Corbusier
1887 Born Charles-Édouard Jeanneret in La-Chaux-de-Fonds in Switzerland
1908/09 Works with the Frères Perret in Paris
1910 Collaborates with Peter Behrens in Berlin
1925 Pavillon de l'Esprit Nouveau at the World Exposition in Paris
1927 Citrohan Haus, Stuttgart
1947–52 Housing settlement Unité d'Habitation in Marseilles
1950–54 Notre Dame du Haut, Ronchamp
1951–56 Chandigarh in northern India is developed following his plans
1953–61 Extension of the La Tourette Monastery in Eveux-sur-Arbresle near Lyon
1963 Carpenter Art Center, Harvard, USA
1965 Dies in Cap-Martin, southern France

"A pilgrimage chapel? It's an arithmetical problem dealing with volumes and quantities!" The architect's enthusiasm for his new commission was not immediate. It was only after the clients had presented convincing arguments that Le Corbusier declared himself prepared to tackle the task, and he was given a free hand in creating a new chapel to take the place of its destroyed predecessor. The celebrated architect was fascinated by two aspects of the project: on the one hand, the harmony between the architecture and the landscape; and, on the other, the complicated requirements of a chapel. A small church for 200 was needed which, twice a year, would become a place of pilgrimage. On 8 September and 15 August, thousands of pilgrims take part in Marian celebrations on the hill above the village of Ronchamp about 20 kilometres (12 miles) from Belfort. The old chapel on the hill witnessed the largest number of pilgrims in 1873, when more than 30,000 believers celebrated the birth of the Virgin Mary – and the end of the Franco-Prussian War – there.

Function and Form

Lying at a height of around 500 metres (1,640 feet) above sea level, the plateau on which the chapel stands provides a secure site in the midst of the green, gently rolling landscape. A chapel had been built there during the Middle Ages. The new chapel, erected between 1950 and 1954, is usually approached from the south: the first sight is of a windowless tower and a protruding, heavy roof resting on a curved white wall. The main entrance, framed on both sides by enamelled steel sheets, is inserted into a straight section of the wall. Le Corbusier was also a painter of abstract pictures and he himself created the design for the main portal. Its lively colours form a contrast to the white plaster. The variously sized window openings seem to be distributed arbitrarily over the outer wall, making it appear to be riddled with holes (their distribution is reminiscent of abstract art). The roof ends at the south-east corner in an upward sweep that suggests the bow of a ship. The external choir, for open-air masses, lies in front of the east wall and is protected by a widely protruding roof. The north wall is dominated by right angles, whereas the western wall is a rounded, windowless surface. The chapel under the brown roof is a dazzling white, but several other sections, such as the pulpit of the external choir and the wall of the entrance portal, are left in bare concrete, as is the pilgrims' hostel with its dormitories and dining rooms, and the custodian's house for the church's chaplain.

The main entrance of the church is faced with enamelled steel sheets

next pages: Notre Dame du Haut, pilgrimage church and architectural icon

44

GUGGENHEIM MUSEUM

A spiral ramp rising over a circular floor plan hardly suggests a museum. However, the Guggenheim Museum, which was completed in 1959, is now one of the most famous museum buildings in the world.

Guggenheim Museum, New York City, USA

1956–59

Frank Lloyd Wright

1867   Born in Richland Center, Wisconsin

1887   Begins work in the architectural office of Louis Henry Sullivan and Dankmar Adler, in Chicago

ca. 1900 Prairie Houses in the suburbs of Chicago

1916–20 Hotel Imperial in Tokyo (destroyed), together with Antonin Raymond

1920s Private houses in California, using prefabricated concrete modules

1935/36 Falling Water House in Bear Run, Pennsylvania

1936–39 Johnson Administration Building in Racine, Wisconsin

1956–59 Guggenheim Museum, New York

1959   Dies in Phoenix, Arizona

In 1943, museum curator Hilla Rebay contacted the architect Frank Lloyd Wright. At the time, the collection of modern art the industrialist Solomon Guggenheim had accumulated was without a suitable exhibition space: "I need a warrior, a lover of space, an organizer, an experimental and wise man … I want a temple of the spirit, a monument", was how the project was explained to the architect. For Wright, the location in New York was anything but inspiring; but, on the other hand, he was attracted to the prospect of building a museum. He presented his plans, not knowing that over the next 15 years, six additional plans with more than 700 drawings would be required.

Architecture as Sculpture

In 1945, the architect and client were in broad agreement, but the economic situation in post-war America meant that things moved very slowly. Not only that: Frank Lloyd Wright had to search for a long time before finding the right builder in George Cohen, who was prepared to undertake avant-garde projects – for the building, which would stand on Fifth Avenue between 88th and 89th Streets, was a radically new design. In essence, it's a pile of round discs that increase in diameter as the building rises. What Frank Lloyd Wright created in the heart of Manhattan, not far from Central Park, was in effect a walk-in sculpture.

What about the Art?

Everything looks very different on the inside. The round forms become accessible as spirals, and a long ramp winds its way along the external wall from the ground floor to the upper storey. A glass dome provides illumination from above. Wright even had advice for visitors: they should take a lift to the very top and then wander down, step by slow step, through the entire collection.

The building was not immediately convincing: critics thought that the art by Kandinsky, Klee and Chagall would be overpowered by the building itself. Willem de Kooning and other artists asked themselves – and the public – how their works could be shown on the curved walls of such an unusual building. However, Wright didn't allow himself to be deterred, even when his building was said to resemble a washing machine: "I have heard so many similar reactions and have decided to simply ignore them." The architect did not live to see the opening of the Guggenheim Museum. Half a year before construction was completed in November 1959, and 16 years after his first sketches, Frank Lloyd Wright died at the age of 92.

The horizontally organized round construction

45

TWA TERMINAL

The idea that sparked his highly original design for the airport terminal came to the Finnish architect Eero Saarinen while he was looking at the leftovers of a grapefruit after breakfast. The inspiration may have been prosaic, but the result was one of his most remarkable and original buildings.

TWA Terminal, New York City, USA
1956–62

Eero Saarinen

The new terminal for the largest of New York airports, John F. Kennedy International, looks much more like a journey into the future than the fruit. Saarinen was originally a sculptor before devoting his passion for experimentation to architecture. "We wanted the passengers passing through the rooms to feel themselves in an environment where each section is the consequence of the previous one and all originate in the same formal universe." This statement by Saarinen is a little more informative, but it still doesn't say anything about the choice of forms – does the building resemble a gargantuan bird rising into the skies with its outspread wings … or is it more like a larger-than-life predatory fish?

The Spirit of Flight

J. F. K. Airport occupies an area of 20 square kilometres (eight square miles) to the east of New York. Even before Saarinen's terminal was built, the airport had seen designs of great architectural variety, for the terminals of various airlines enlivened the central building. When Trans World Airlines commissioned the Finnish architect, they gave him carte blanche – his plan had convinced them. A concrete dish made of four arches forms the astonishing roof of the building, with rows of windows nestling beneath these "wings". The roof construction is supported by Y-form supports, whose lines continue in the curved lines of the roof bowl. In the 12,000 square metres (129,200 square feet) of the interior, everything – from the desks to the notice boards – seems to be in movement, precisely capturing the character of an airport.

The airline company let the implementation of Saarinen's plans for a building of glass and concrete cost them $15 m. Sadly, the architect did not live to see the opening of his terminal; he died almost one year before its completion. Not, however, without leaving a poetic note behind – he had wanted, he said, to capture "the spirit of flight" in his design for the terminal. Saarinen's architectural sculpture could not keep pace with the rapid boom in air transport for very long, however, for the demands placed on the terminal changed soon after its completion. Since 1960, the number of passengers at J. F. K. airport has increased fourfold, which has made a series of alterations to the building necessary. There are limits to change, however: the TWA Terminal was named a protected monument in 1994.

"The Spirit of Flight" – the TWA Terminal at John F. Kennedy International Airport

46

CONGRESS BUILDING BRASÍLIA

By the middle of the 20th century, Brazil was well on its way to becoming a modern industrialized nation, a fact that its political leaders felt had to be expressed in its urban architecture. The precise central point of the gigantic country was calculated and a new capital city was planned to emerge just there, on a distant, sparsely populated plateau in the very heart of the country.

Congress Building, Brasília, Brazil
1958–60

Oscar Niemeyer

1907 Born 15 December in Rio de Janeiro

1930–34 Studies architecture at the Academy of Fine Arts, Rio de Janeiro

1936–43 Works on Ministry of Education with Le Corbusier

1946 Boavista Bank, Rio de Janeiro

1956–61 Works as chief architect of Brasília

1964 Goes into exile because of military dictatorship in Brazil

1967 PCF Centre, Paris

1969 Renault headquarters, Paris; Constantine University, Algeria

1983/84 Samba Stadium, Rio de Janeiro

1988 Wins Pritzker Prize

1989 Cultural Centre, São Paulo

1996 Museum of Modern Art, Rio de Janeiro

2002 Casino in Funchal, Madeira

2012 Dies 5 December in Rio de Janeiro

In a way, Brasília – a planned city, built of concrete in a tropical climate – was intended to be a kind of welcoming gift for the new President Juscelino Kubitschek de Oliveira. Brasília could not be expected to supplant the lively and well-established old capital, Rio de Janeiro, located 1,000 kilometres (620 miles) away. But, by the year 2000, more than two million inhabitants lived in the new city, which had been planned for only 500,000. Their enthusiasm for the artificially created city, however, has its limits. There is a common saying among Brazilians that the most attractive view of Brasília is seen on the flight to Rio!

Technology and Tempo

The new city is sited at an altitude of 1,150 metres (3,770 feet) above sea level. The urban planners Lucio Costa and Oscar Niemeyer were largely responsible for its development. They began with their plans for the no-man's-land in 1957, and in only three years, 80,000 workers had created the new centre of the country out of nothing – the only demand the President placed on his planning team was the city had to be built as quickly as possible. The city was officially dedicated in 1960.

The remote area had offered the planners one great advantage: they didn't have to take existing buildings or sites into consideration, so it was possible to create something completely new quickly. The layout of Brasília is in the form of an airplane – it's hardly possible to express the belief in progress and technology more clearly. For all its straightforward functionalism, Niemeyer's architecture is rich in symbolism.

Significant Features

"It was always important for me that my buildings have something surprising about them, that they invent something previously unseen." There can be no question that Niemeyer relished the surprising moments in the numerous civic buildings he erected in a line along the north-south axis. Among these governmental and cultural buildings we find government ministries, the university, the congress building, and its neighbours on the "Square of the Three Forces", the Supreme Court and the presidential palace. A high-rise building housing the representatives' offices towers above a low building that is home to the House of Representatives and the Senate. The scene is dominated by straight lines and right angles, and the façades are sheathed in glass. All very modern. Two huge bowls lie resplendent on the flat roofs: one forms the dome of the Senate (and so suggests containment), the other, upturned and open above, sits on the roof of the House of Representatives (representing a container for the votes of the people). The views of the surrounding country that can be seen from this building are no less impressive.

The towers of the Supreme Administration Authority

next pages: Overall view of the Congress Building

47

SYDNEY OPERA HOUSE

Not far from Sydney, a small peninsula, known as Bennelong Point, juts into the bay. Inspired by this strip of land between city and sea, the Danish architect Jørn Utzon created a highly original and once controversial opera house that soon became the proud symbol of Sydney – a confidently modern image for a city increasingly affluent and cosmopolitan.

Sydney Opera House, Australia
1957–73

Jørn Utzon

1918 Born 9 April in Copenhagen
1942 Completes his architecture studies at the Copenhagen Academy of Arts
1946 Works with Alvar Aalto in Helsinki
1947/48 Travels through Europe, Morocco and Mexico
1950 Becomes a freelance architect
1956 Wins international attention with his prize-winning plans for the Sydney Opera House
1959 Melli Bank, Teheran
1963 Museum in Silkeborg, Denmark
1983 Parliament Building in Kuwait
2003 Wins Pritzker Prize
2008 Dies 29 November 2008 near Copenhagen

When the city announced the competition for an opera house in 1956, the intention was to provide seating for 7,000 people and to have two main halls: a large one for symphonic concerts, opera and ballet, and a smaller one for theatrical performances, chamber music and readings. Utzon, who won the competition from among 222 participants, met these conditions and with a striking design – though from the outside there's no telling precisely what's happening on the inside!

An Opera House as Sculpture

Visitors reach the various halls by climbing broad flights of steps that lead up to the concrete platform on which the complex stands. The smallest of the three "shells" stands over a restaurant. The next in size contains the opera house, and the largest houses both the concert hall and (below that) a small theatre. From the exterior, the shell-like roofs dominate completely. These remarkable structures, reminiscent of shells or sails (both perfectly in keeping with its harbourside setting), give the building a highly sculpted appearance. Their curved surfaces are covered with large glazed ceramic tiles that shine a brilliant white in the Australian sun.

And Utzon was concerned not just with what the visitors heard, but also with what they saw: the Opera House is located on a platform 15 metres (49 feet) high that provides breath-taking views of the harbour and coastline. The building is surrounded by water on three sides – its closest neighbours are not houses and office blocks but boats and ships.

Risk and Success

The reaction to his winning design could hardly have been more varied, ranging from "sheer poetry" to "a Danish pastry". And it was not only the critical reaction that was a risk: technically, the building pushed the boundaries of what was possible at the time. The leading engineer Ove Orup was responsible for constructing the innovative shell structures. Ten thousand workers from 28 countries worked on the building between 1959 and 1973, and in 1962 Utzon moved to Sydney to oversee progress. And there were problems that had nothing to do with design or the technology. During the turbulent 1960s, various social movements used the most prominent building site in Australia to publicise their demonstrations; the workers went on strike for better conditions and pay; and members of the ecological movement challenged the project's environmental impact on the bay.

But construction progressed and the roof was completed in 1967. However, Utzon was back in his distant homeland by this stage. One year before, he had withdrawn from the project and returned to Denmark – costs had skyrocketed since construction had begun and Utzon was in a catastrophic financial situation. His successors completed work on the building in 1973. It was not until 2000 that Utzon – then 82 – finally accepted the Australian government's request to continue working on the upkeep and improvement of the interior of his masterpiece.

The Sydney Opera House, the city's symbol

next pages: The Opera House is located on a small tongue of land between the harbour and the city centre

48

OLYMPIC PARK IN MUNICH

"Faster, higher, stronger?" A definite "deeper!" was added to this sporting motto for the Olympic Games in Munich in 1972 – two-thirds of the Olympic Stadium is located underground in a deep depression in the landscape.

Olympic Park, Munich, Germany
1968–72

Günter Behnisch
1922 Born in Lockwitz near Dresden
1947–51 Studies architecture at the Technical University in Stuttgart
1952 Sets up an architectural studio with Bruno Lambart
1967–72 Olympic Park, Munich
1973–80 Reconstruction of the Schlossplatz (Castle Square) and Königsstrasse in Stuttgart
1987 Library of the Catholic University, Eichstätt
1990 Museum for Post and Communication, Frankfurt am Main
1992 Bundestag Building, Bonn
2001 Buchheim Museum Bernried
2008 Deutscher Kritikerpreis (cultural prize)
2010 Dies 12 July in Stuttgart

A park landscape with no intrusive buildings was the aim for Munich. Those who commissioned the stadium wanted an Olympic Games in the countryside. The intention was to create a counterpart to the Olympic Stadium in Berlin, where the Games in 1936 were used primarily as a demonstration of political power. So to avoid too powerful an impression, only one-third of the Munich Olympic Stadium was erected above ground; two-thirds was built below the surface. The challenge of working with a limited number of materials was met with the curved roof that quickly became the symbol of the 1972 Summer Olympics.

The "Tent"

The ultramodern "net construction" technique that made it possible to span large areas had emerged in the 1950s, and the engineer Frei Otto developed the membrane structure further. At Munich, the net of translucent acrylic glass sheets, which measures a vast 74,800 square metres (805,140 square feet), forms a tent-like structure that stretches over the landscape and buildings, the western section of the Olympic Stadium, the Olympic Hall, and the swimming arena. This roof is supported by only 12 pylons, the highest of which measures 81 metres (266 feet), and 36 smaller round supports. This is possible because the weight is carried by steel cables and cement blocks set deep into the ground.

Not all experts were convinced that the design would work, as they considered the enormous span of the net construction "tent" to be far too large. But it was successful, though there was one problem: the covering of the roof cost ten times the original (already substantial) estimate! The issue was hotly debated by the chief architect, Günter Behnisch, and the Olympic Building Consortium (OBG), which consisted of the federal government and the state government. To his claim that he had "designed a Volkswagen and the OBG turned it into a Cadillac", they replied that "Behnisch planned a Cadillac and thought he could power it with a Volkswagen engine".

Today

Whether a Cadillac or a Volkswagen, the Olympic Park, which was laid out in northern Munich between 1968 and 1972, is still in use today. Covering three square kilometres (1.2 square miles), this large recreational area is now used for numerous sporting and cultural events. It's no problem to climb the 60 metres (197 feet) of the Olympic Hill, but the 290 metres (950 feet) of the Olympia Tower – the highest reinforced concrete construction in Europe – is more demanding. The Nymphenburg Canal was turned into the Olympia Lake, and the Stadium, with its 57,450 seats and standing room for 12,000, is used for concerts today. Moreover, the former Olympic Village has become home to around 9,000 residents.

This former parade ground, which was later used as Munich's first airport, and even as a dump for rubble after the Second World War, has finally become an integral part of the city's landscape.

The roof landscape of the Olympic Park quotes the shoreline of the Olympic Lake

49

JEWISH MUSEUM BERLIN

Daniel Libeskind was already a professional musician when his interest in architecture awoke. The extension to the museum to commemorate 2,000 years of German-Jewish history, which he built in the Berlin suburb of Kreuzberg, was his first major project – and it proved controversial and deeply moving.

Jewish Museum Berlin, Germany
1992–99

Daniel Libeskind
1946 Born in Poland
1965 Granted American citizenship Studies music in Israel and New York
1970 Completes his architectural studies at the Cooper Union for the Advancement of Science and Art in New York
1989 Wins the competition for the construction of the Jewish Museum Berlin
1995–98 Felix Nussbaum Haus, City Museum Osnabrück
1999 Wins German Architectural Prize for the Jewish Museum
2003 Wins the competition for the World Trade Center site at Ground Zero in New York
2006 Extension of the Denver Art Museum
2010 Bord Gáis Energy Theatre, Dublin
2011 Reflections at Keppel Bay in Singapore; Military History Museum Dresden and Run Run Shaw Creative Media Centre in Hong Kong
2015 Vanke Pavilion, Milan
2018 MO Modern Art Museum, Vilnius

Seen from the outside, the Jewish Museum consists of two very different buildings. The visitor is initially greeted by a Baroque, three-winged building in cheerful yellow. This two-storey building was erected in 1730 by Johann Philipp Gerlach, and originally served as a courthouse under Frederick William I. Since 2001, it has been part of the research and documents centre on Jewish history. Commissioned for the Museum's permanent exhibition, the new building, with its stark, irregular metallic forms, stands out strongly against its elegant Baroque neighbour.

Between the Lines

This ultra-modern extension, built on a zigzag ground plan, is covered with silver-grey sheets of zinc and is cut open with a series of slit-like windows. Designed by Daniel Libeskind, this building, which is connected to the older one by an underground flight of stairs, is initially very perplexing to its many visitors, for the more familiar arrangement of rooms and passageways has been abandoned. Some of the floors slope, there are strangely angled corners, and many areas are in semi-darkness. Libeskind wanted to create what he called underground "streets", a series of passageways, each leading to a different part of the building. Even the shell of the building attracted masses of visitors: 350,000 visited the still-empty building. Since then, more than 3.5 million visitors have wandered through the tortuous structure.

"The official name of the project is 'Jewish Museum', but I called it 'Between the Lines', because, in my opinion, we are dealing with two lines, two flows of consciousness, organization and connections. One line is straight, but split into many fragments, the other winds its way and continues on eternally", was how the architect described it.

Rich in Symbolism

At the point where these two lines meet there are five empty spaces called "Voids", which, with their naked concrete walls, represent the emptiness left by the Holocaust. The subterranean passageways lead to the various main areas of the exhibition. The first and longest of the three is the "Axis of Continuity", which leads steeply upwards into the two floors of the permanent exhibition. The "Axis of Emigration", on the other hand, guides the visitor to the outside along a corridor that becomes increasingly narrow between its slightly slanting walls. In an underground garden, there is an area containing 49 huge white pillars, filled with earth, out of which trees grow. The third axis, the "Axis of the Holocaust", draws the visitor into a dark passage in which there is a heavy steel door that closes with a heavy thud: behind this lies the 24-metre (79-feet) high Holocaust Tower – a cold, dark, completely empty space dedicated to the memory of the Jewish victims of the Holocaust.

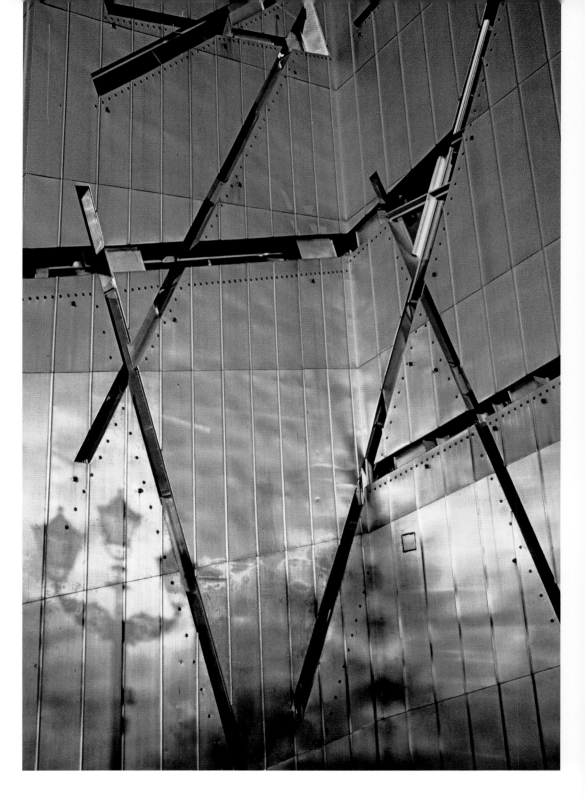

Zinc sheets and slit-like rows of windows characterize the external appearance of the Museum

One of the three axes

The Garden of Steles

50

NATIONAL STADIUM IN BEIJING

With seats for 91,000 spectators the sporting events were presented in Beijing's Olympic Stadium, the "Bird's Nest". This spectacular arena for the 29th Summer Olympic Games, which was held in 2008, was designed by the Swiss architects Herzog & de Meuron, in collaboration with local Chinese architects.

National Stadium, Beijing, China
2003–08

Architects Herzog & de Meuron, Basel, Switzerland
Engineering and Sports Architecture China Architectural Design & Research Group, Beijing, China
Ove Arup & Partners Hong Kong Ltd., Kowloon, Hong Kong
Arup Sports, London, United Kingdom
Artistic Consultation Ai Weiwei, Beijing, China

Jacques Herzog & Pierre de Meuron
1950   Both born in Basel
1970–75 Study Architecture at the Federal Institute of Technology (ETH) Zurich
1978   Start their collaboration
1987   Ricola Warehouse, Laufen
Since 1999 Professorship at the ETH, Zurich
2000   Tate Modern, London
2001   Win Pritzker Prize.
2003   Prada Aoyama Epicenter, Tokyo. Schaulager Laurenz-Foundation, Basel. Laban Creekside, London. Trinity Laban Dance Centre, London.
2005   Allianz Arena, Munich, Walker Art Center, Minneapolis. de Young Museum, San Francisco
2007–17 Elbphilharmonie, Hamburg

The Olympic Games in Beijing provided many opportunities to create spectacular new and innovative buildings; the challenge was how to integrate them into the existing city. Following the master plan by Sasaki Associates, who won the competition to develop the Olympic Site, the sporting facilities flank the axis that runs through the Chinese capital – from Forest Park in the north, past the Forbidden City, to Tiananmen Square in the south – thereby linking nature, sport and culture. The northern end of the axis forms the core area for the Games. Here the buildings are embedded in generous green areas, hills, woods and biotopes, and the city landscape is interspersed with numerous pools and lakes. Work on the new Olympic Stadium began in 2003, around the cube-shaped swimming centre.

The "Bird's Nest"

The design for the stadium was nicknamed the "bird's nest" at the very beginning, the name greatly appealing to the Swiss architects. They described their office as a laboratory where the "processes of nature are imitated". They employed 240 professionals from 25 countries who worked on 40 parallel projects. And indeed this remarkable structure, a vast bowl, resembled a bird's nest. For the architects, it satisfied four conditions: it's a fully contemporary Chinese building, it exploits the advantages of modern technology, it respects its natural environment, and it has close links with traditional Chinese culture. The longitudinal axis extends over 320 metres (1,049 feet) and the width is 297.3 metres (975 feet). This monumental bird's nest sits raised on a base platform that made it possible to do without excavating a foundation.

Who Needs a Roof?

This remarkable building consists of long, interwoven members that create a vast, net-like structure that is self-supporting. In the same way as birds line their nests with material, the architects have closed the open surfaces of the exterior with a transparent membrane that allows for ventilation. In this design, façade and structure are identical. The fact that this structure is self-supporting means that there are no pillars in the 69-metre (226-feet) high interior to prevent the sporting fans from having an unobstructed view of their sporting heroes – the field of vision is unrestricted in all directions.

Just a year after they had begun, the architects had to abandon the original plan to cover the interior entirely with a transparent sliding roof. The costs had already greatly exceeded early estimates. However, the new roof design also provided a worthy covering for the track-and-field events, the football tournament and, of course, the elaborate opening and closing ceremonies of the Olympics in the Far East.

Net-like construction: Façade and load-bearing structure are one and the same

GLOSSARY

Art Deco

A decorative style of the 1920s and 1930s, characterised by elegant but simple forms (in contrast to the linear richness of Art Nouveau), bold colours and the use of precious materials such as lacquer, ivory, marble, chrome etc. It was named after an exhibition of applied arts held in Paris in 1925.

Art Nouveau

Around 1900, when science and technology were developing rapidly, many architects, sculptors and painters, as well as carpenters, glaziers and jewellers, looked back to the traditional craftsmanship of past centuries. They were passionate about sweeping lines and decorative ornaments. The movement had different names in different countries: Jugendstil, Art Nouveau or Modernism. The appearance of Barcelona was transformed by Antoní Gaudí, Lluis Domènech i Montaner, and others. They integrated a great variety of stylistic quotations into their residential buildings, parks and public buildings, and used mosaics, glazed ceramics and other craft techniques to created colourful, asymmetrical designs strongly influenced by nature, and in particular by plant forms.

Baroque

The Baroque period was the age of political absolutism and, therefore, of the conspicuous display of power, opulence and wealth. The secular and religious worlds were closely linked; the splendour of the churches and monasteries in Europe is in no way different from that of the palaces. The architectural design, all interior décor, and often even the landscape in which the building was set were elements of the Baroque "total work of art". Stretching from around 1600 to the middle of the 18th century, the Baroque style developed throughout Europe, though often with clear national differences. The decorative but much lighter style known as Rococo emerged from late Baroque during the 18th century.

Basilica

(Greek *basiliké*: "king's hall") In antiquity, a grand, hall-like public building consisting of a long central section (nave) flanked by two aisles that are separated from the nave by rows of columns. The nave is wider and considerably higher than the two side aisles. The basilica became one of the most important forms of early Christian and mediaeval church building. In its church form, an altar niche (the apse) is usually attached to the eastern end of the nave.

Central-plan Building

A building in which the main axes radiate from a central point. This means that the possible layouts are circular, oval, square, cross-shaped, octagonal or polygonal. The central room can be surrounded by a gallery and/or open onto chapels, niches and other adjacent rooms. One of the oldest preserved central-plan buildings is the Pantheon in Rome.

Choir

The altar area at the east end of a church, originally reserved for the clergy. Initially separated from the rest of the church by a chancel screen, over time it developed its own distinctive architectural form and decoration (such as choir stalls). Among its special features are the ambulatory (an extension of the side aisles around the choir) and choir chapels.

Column

A perpendicular building support (of wood, stone or metal) with a round cross-section – this distinguishes it from half-columns, pillars and pilasters. In contrast to a pillar, a column does not necessarily play a structural role: it can be merely decorative. Columns can also be free-standing monuments: a well-known example is Nelson's Column in London. A column's structure and decoration are based on the three main classical forms: Doric, Ionic and Corinthian. See below.

Corinthian Column

The last of the three classical orders to develop, and the most elaborate. Its base and shaft are generally similar to those of the Ionic column (see next page). The biggest differences are found in the capital: the number of volutes topping the capital is increased from two to eight, but they are greatly reduced in size and seldom project far over the side of the column. The scrolls grow out of stylized acanthus leaves arranged in two rows, one above the other.

Doric Column

The oldest (and simplest) of the three classical architectural orders. In contrast to the Ionic and Corinthian orders, the Doric column has no base, which means that the column begins immediately with its shaft, which is fluted (decorated with vertical grooves) and is thicker than those of an Ionic or Corinthian columns. The capital is small, plain and round, and crowned with a square slab called an abacus.

Frieze

Initially part of the entablature in Greek temples, a frieze late became a long, horizontal band on a wall, internal or external, carrying painted or carved ornaments or figural representations. Architecturally, a frieze serves to articulate a large expanse of wall.

Giant (or Colossal) Order

A classical building design in which columns, pillars or pilasters stretch over two or more storeys. The Colossal order was used to make a façade far more impressive.

Gothic

Around the middle of the 12th century, something new developed out of the heavy forms of Romanesque architecture. Cathedrals became higher, round arches became pointed, ceilings were constructed of arched vaults supported by slender ribs, and externally buttresses were used to support the walls. These basic structural elements created a strong framework that carried the weight of the building. Now freed from this task, the walls could be pierced by windows, flooding the interior with brightly coloured light. The Gothic style, which originated in France, soon spread to England, Germany, the Netherlands, Spain and Italy, and in one form or another endured until about 1500.

Ionic Column

One of the three classical architectural orders, more ornate than Doric but simpler than Corinthian. The foundation is formed by a square base plate (plinth) on which rest several rounded bands. The column itself is fluted, and the capital is often formed by a horizontal band of finely carved decoration that sits between two large volutes scrolling down on each side.

Neo-Classicism

A style in art and architecture, flourishing c.1770–1840, that was a reaction to the light, playful, organic forms of the Rococo period. Based on a return to the architecture of classical antiquity, it employed characteristic elements of Greek and Roman design, notably columns, pediments and porticoes. The emphasis was on order, proportion, a restrained grandeur and a sometimes austere simplicity. By the middle of the 18th century, Italy – and Rome in particular – had become the source of inspiration for artists, architects, writers and political thinkers. The Brandenburg Gate in Berlin, the Arc de Triomphe in Paris, the British Museum in London, and the Capitol in Washington are among the most famous Neo-Classical buildings.

Loggia

(Italian: "columned hall") A part of a building open on at least one side, which, in contrast to the portico or balcony, does not protrude beyond the building's profile. The open sides are often supported by slender columns. Loggias were particularly popular in the palaces of the Italian Renaissance.

Mannerism

The dominant style of the period between the Renaissance and Baroque in painting, architecture, sculpture, music and literature, c.1520–1620. The term was introduced by Giorgio Vasari in reference to Michelangelo ("maniera di Michelangelo"). It is characterised by the renunciation of the harmonious and balanced compositions of the Renaissance in favour of tense, expressive works full of emotion, unrest and exaggerated elegance. The Escorial near Madrid is an important architectural example, and El Greco and Jacopo da Pontormo were prominent Mannerist painters.

Minimalism

An art movement that developed in painting, sculpture and design in the 1960s. Rejecting the intense emotionalism and subjectivism of such movements as Abstract Expressionism, Minimalism sought an impersonal art, typically employing commercially produced, geometrical products (such as steel cubes) arranged in rows or series. Donald Judd, Carl André and Dan Flavin are among the most important artists of this movement. More generally, Minimalism describes forms of architecture or design that are stripped to bare essentials.

Obelisk

(Latin obeliscus, Greek obelískos: "pointed column") A four-sided, tapering stone column in the form of a very slender pyramid, used as a solitarily standing monument.

Orangerie

Originally, an exotic collection of citrus trees at European courts in the 16th century. In time, the term was used of the buildings or rooms used to protect the trees. Often elegantly designed, these were frequently used for social events.

Pantheon

(Greek pan: "all" and theós: "god") In ancient Greece, a sanctuary dedicated to "all the gods". Over time, this meaning expanded and today the term is generally used of a monument honouring a country's illustrious dead. The oldest preserved building of this kind is the Pantheon in Rome, which was erected under Emperor Hadrian in the 2nd century AD.

Renaissance

The Italian 16th-century art historian Giorgio Vasari was the first to speak of a Rinascimento – a "rebirth" or Renaissance – of the arts. For him, this was the flowering of art after what he saw as the gloom of the Middle Ages. The term Renaissance is now used to describe the era's painting, sculpture, architecture, philosophy and literature. It was a culture characterized by a return to the works of antiquity, a passion for perspective, and, last but not least, a completely new understanding of man as the summit of creation. The Italian Renaissance had its origins in 15th-century Florence.

Relief

A sculpture in which the forms project from a flat surface (of stone, wood, metal or ivory). Reliefs were often used to decorate the surfaces of buildings, such as the walls (internal and external), pediments and church portals. They were particularly popular in ancient Greece and Rome, and also Renaissance Italy.

Romanesque

The characteristic art and architecture of France, Spain, Italy, Germany and England from around 1000 to 1250 was Romanesque. Introduced in the 19th century, this term was intended to describe a return to the building forms of ancient Rome. Even though there are marked regional differences in the architecture of the Romanesque, there are some important common features, notably round (Norman) arches, and thick walls with small windows. In the Romanesque era, the basilica, essentially a long nave with broad side aisles, became the preferred form for church construction. Many Romanesque churches and monasteries were richly decorated with sculptures and ornaments. The principal secular buildings during this era were castles and palaces.

Spolia

(Latin spolium: "booty, something taken from the enemy") Building elements plundered from older buildings (especially those of antiquity) in order to be reused in a later building. Typically columns, sculptures, friezes, capitals, architraves, lintels etc. Originally, old buildings were exploited simply because they provided an inexpensive source of building material. In time, however, the cultural references made by the spolia became increasingly important.

Stupa

(Sanskrit stup: "pile up, accumulate") Originally, a round mound of earth built up over a grave. Within a few centuries, this simple burial mound developed into the basic form of the classical Buddhist stupa: a square platform on which sits a hemispheric dome surmounted by a crown and spire. The oldest construction of this kind, found in Sanchi in Central India, was built in the third century BC.

Tracery

The ornate stone ribbing in the windows of Gothic churches. Its basic purpose is structural – it supports large areas of glass – but it also has an important decorative function. It developed during the High Gothic era in France and reached its peak in the English Perpendicular Style.

Transept

In a church, one of the short "arms" that intersects the nave at the east end, near the altar, usually aligned north-south.

INDEX

PHOTO CREDITS

iStock.com/Akis Papadopoulos: pp. 8/9; Hervé Champollion: p. 11, 103; LOOK: pp. 12/13, 15, 69, 91, 97, 100/101, 105, 113; iStock.com/outcast85: p. 21; iStock.com/THPStock: p. 23; iStock.com/Ozbalci: p. 25; Knut Liese: pp. 26/27; iStock.com/Flavio Vallenari: p. 29; Vladimir Zhoga/Shutterstock.com: p. 31; Bildarchiv Monheim: pp. 33, 150; Takashi Images/Shutterstock.com: p. 34; Uwe Aranas/Shutterstock.com: p. 35; Adel Newman/Shutterstock.com: p. 37; Botond Horvath/ Shutterstock.com: p. 39; LAIF: pp. 40/41, 59, 81, 91, 115, 127; Markus Hilbich: p. 43; A. F. Kersting: pp. 45; iStock.com/Hanis: pp. 46/47; JBE Photo: pp. 49, 50/51; iStock.com/

istankov: p. 53; iStock.com/Mauro_Repossini: pp. 54/55; Bildagentur Huber, GAP: p. 61; Stella Christiansen: pp. 62/63; iStock.com/ET1972: p. 65; iStock.com/Mauro_Repossini: pp. 66/67; iStock.com/Pel_1971: pp. 70/71; Constanze von Witzleben: p. 73; iStock.com/Randrey: pp. 74/75; Irina Mos/Shutterstock.com: p. 77; Bildagentur Huber, GAP/Giovanni Simeone: pp. 78/79; Peter Stepan: pp. 82/83; Martin Thomas: p. 85; Bilderberg: p. 87; iStock.com/Mlenny: p. 89; iStock.com/Chuyu: p. 91; Jose Ignacio Soto/Shutterstock.com: p. 93; akg-images: pp. 94/95; Achim Bednorz: p. 99; stock.adobe.com/Colin & Linda McKie: p. 107;

iStock.com/Kirkikis: p. 109; Marcus Brooke: pp. 110/111; B.O'Kane / Alamy Stock Foto: p. 117; Hans Engels: pp. 119-121; Jörg Machirus: pp. 123-125; Norman McGrath: p. 129; Oleg Mitiukhin / Alamy Stock Foto: pp. 132/133; Rainer Grosskopf: p. 135; Werner Neumeister: p. 136; iStock.com/Meinzahn: p. 137; Paul Springett C / Alamy Stock Foto: p. 139; iStock.com/diegograndi: pp. 140/141; iStock.com/hatman12: p. 143; iStock.com/JulieanneBirch: pp. 144/145; Tichr/Shutterstock.com: p. 147; Dirk Radzinski: p. 149; Florian Profitlich: p. 151; iStock.com/PhotoTalk: p. 153

IMPRINT

Cover: Jørn Utzon, Sydney Opera House, 1957 – 73, Copyright: georgeclerk/Getty Images; Taj Mahal, 1632 – 52, Copyright: akg-images/Horizons/Jochem Wijnands
Frontispiece: William van Alen, Chrysler Building, New York, 1928 – 30, Copyright: Corbis, Düsseldorf/Richard Hamilton Smith

© Prestel Verlag, Munich · London · New York 2007, reprinted 2019
A member of Verlagsgruppe Random House GmbH, Neumarkter Straße 28 · 81673 Munich

© for the works reproduced is held by the architects and artists, their heirs or assigns, with the exception of: Walter Gropius with VG Bild-Kunst, Bonn 2019; Le Corbusier with FLC/VG Bild-Kunst, Bonn 2019; Frank Lloyd Wright with Frank Lloyd Wright Foundation/VG Bild-Kunst, Bonn 2019; Ludwig Mies van der Rohe with VG Bild-Kunst, Bonn 2019

Prestel Publishing Ltd.
14 – 17 Wells Street
London W1T 3PD

Prestel Publishing
900 Broadway, Suite 603
New York, NY 10003

Library of Congress Control Number is available; a CIP catalogue record for this book is available from the British Library.

Project management: Katharina Haderer, Claudia Stäuble
Relaunch: Stella Christiansen
Copy-editing: Reegan Finger, Chris Murray, Jane Michael
Cover design: Sofarobotnik
Typesetting: ew print & medien service gmbh
Production: Andrea Cobré
Printing and binding: DZS Grafik, d.o.o., Ljubljana

Verlagsgruppe Random House FSC ®N001967

Printed in Slovenia on 150g Primaset

ISBN 978-3-7913-8588-4

www.prestel.com

THE GREAT PYRAMID OF GIZA
2554 – 2531 BC

KARNAK TEMPLE
1550 – 715 BC

THE PARTHENON
447 – 432 BC

PETRA
100 BC – AD 200

THE COLOSSEUM
72 – 80 AD

TIKAL
2ND – 9TH C AD

HAGIA SOPHIA
AD 532 – 537

SAN VITALE
AD 526 – 547

HORYUJI TEMPLE
7TH C AD

PALATINE CHAPEL IN AACHEN
AD 790

BOROBUDUR
AD 800

THE MEZQUITA
FROM AD 785

THE HRADČANY
9TH C AD

DURHAM CATHEDRAL
FROM 1093

ANGKOR WAT
12TH C

NOTRE-DAME
FROM 1163

CASTEL DEL MONTE
CA. 1240

WESTMINSTER ABBEY
FROM 1245

THE FORBIDDEN CITY
1406 – 21

THE DOGE'S PALACE
FROM 1340

CATHEDRAL DOME IN FLORENCE
1418 – 36

THE KREMLIN
FROM 1156

ST PETER'S BASILICA
FROM 1506

CHÂTEAU OF CHAMBORD
FROM 1519

MACHU PICCHU
15TH C

VILLA LA ROTONDA
FROM 1566

2554 BC – 790 AD   800 – 1240   1245 – 1566

TIMELINE